Here they are --
Amos 'n' Andy

By

CHARLES J. CORRELL

FREEMAN F. GOSDEN

Foreword by
IRVIN S. COBB

RAY LONG &
RICHARD R. SMITH, INC.
NEW YORK   1931

Copyright, 1931, by
CHARLES J. CORRELL AND FREEMAN F. GOSDEN
All rights reserved

*Printed in the United States of America
by Harris Wolff Estate, New York*

Amos: Whut is you goin' figger?

Andy: I got figger whut kind o' job I wants an' whut kind o' job I got git you. Lemme see yere—you kin do de heavy work 'cause you ain't got much sense as I is.

FOREWORD
By Irvin S. Cobb

Since they attained a national importance and a national popularity without precedent or parallel even in these piping radio times, our friends, Amos 'n' Andy, have been the subject of countless speculations on the part of those who profess to be students of what is called mob-psychology.

Some of the wise ones have said it was all due to the fact that their work was to the microphone what the "comic strip" is to the daily paper—a carrying-forward day after day of the same characters, the same thread of continuing interest, the same semblance to a humorous plot.

Whereas others have been equally cocksure in the assertion that the enormous success of the thing sprang out of its "novelty"—as though any form of entertainment which happens to be a little bit different is not, at the beginning, a novelty; and they have kept on offering this feeble diagnosis months and years after the amusing adventures of Amos 'n' Andy ceased to be novelties and became fixtures in the public mind.

For an amazing phenomenon which stands on its own merits and needs neither explanation nor analysis I'd like to offer my own modest theory even though it happens to be the theory which many others before me have offered. I claim these two stout fellows won a place in the popular taste and have held it against all comers because they are so natural, so simple, so full of an unforced joyousness, so doggoned human.

In their broadcasted dialogues as they come to me and to millions of others over the evening air I never yet have been able to detect any effort to be earnestly creative or even any attempt at pure originality. What I do feel is that Amos 'n' Andy merely are a couple of genuine, orthodox, true-to-type, flesh-and-blood Afro-Americans who, in their naïve generosity, have extended to me the pleasant boon of being able to listen in on them while they live their lives and have their successes and their failures, their ups and their downs—but more downs than ups.

In this book, the first published compilation of Amos 'n' Andy's little tales, starting with their start in the South and carrying them along through their first crowded months in the big town, the same spirit, the same essences, the same authenticity and genuineness of the radio are caught in type and preserved between covers.

And, golly, what grand dialect they use! It's perfect, I say—absolutely perfect.

The present volume needs no foreword from me, no word of praise. But because I think these boys have done a grand job and because I've found a laugh for myself in every page I'm very glad and very proud to do this little introduction for the first of their literary endeavors.

I

Amos and Andy, two lifelong buddies from Dixie, have spent most of their life on a farm just outside Atlanta, Ga. Amos is a hard-working little fellow who tries to do everything he can to help others and to make himself progress while his friend Andy is not especially fond of hard work and often has Amos assist him in his own duties. As the curtain goes up, we find the boys returning to the farmhouse with a bucket of milk—both are enthusiastic about going to Chicago where they have heard good, high-salaried jobs are available. *Here they are*:

AMOS: I wuz sittin' yere dreamin' 'bout Chicago an' 'stead o' puttin' de milk in de bucket, I put half of it on de ground.
ANDY: Dat's whut you git fur not tendin' to yore bizness. If I'd been milkin' dat cow, son, I wouldn't of wasted a drop o' milk.
AMOS: When I tell Mister Hopkins dat I lost half de milk, he goin' git mad wid me.
ANDY: Let him git mad wid you. You ain't got no bizness shootin' de milk on de ground.
AMOS: I got tell him though 'cause he knows I ought to have mo' milk dan dis.
ANDY: Instead o' payin' 'tention to whut you was doin', you was sittin' dere dreamin'.
AMOS: Yeah—if I hadn't been thinkin' 'bout goin' to

Chicago den, I'd of got de milk in de bucket a'right.

ANDY: Well, it's yore own fault—dat's all I got say.

AMOS: You know, YOU wuz de one he tol' to milk de cow.

ANDY: Dat IS right, ain't it?

AMOS: He tol' you to milk de cow—he didn't tell me to do it. You is de one dat's got take de milk in to him.

ANDY: On second thought, yere, we better not tell him nothin' 'bout losin' part o' de milk 'cause I don' want him jumpin' all over me.

AMOS: Well, whut you goin' do 'bout it? We ought to tell him. Dat's de right thing to do.

ANDY: Wait a minute, yere, son. I got a idea.

AMOS: Whut you goin' to do now?

ANDY: Come on over yere wid me. Han' me dat bucket.

AMOS: Where you goin'? Whut you goin' do wid it?

ANDY: Yere's de well right yere. We'll fill dat up wid water.

AMOS: Wait a minute—you can't do dat wid de stuff. Dat's goin' make Mister Hopkins mad if he ever find dat out.

ANDY: How he goin' find it out?

AMOS: He's li'ble to find it out though. We ain't got no bizness puttin' water in de milk.

ANDY: Now, lissen yere, Amos—don't never try to tell me whut to do or whut not to do. I know whut I'se doin'.

AMOS: I know, but if Mister Hopkins ever see you doin' dat, he's li'ble to fire both of us.

ANDY: Hol' dat bucket o' milk dere while I pour some water in it.

Amos: I don' wants to git mixed up in dis. I ain't goin' do it. De man don' want no water in his milk.

Andy: Do whut I tell you to do now an' don' gimme no backtalk. Hadn't been fo' me, we wouldn't of had dis job.

Amos: Well, I'll hold de bucket den, but I certainly do hate to put water in de man's milk.

Andy: Hold it still now.

Amos: I think you got enough in dere now, Andy.

Andy: Shut up now—I know whut I'se doin'.

Amos: Wait a minute yere—you got too much water in dere.

Andy: Dat IS a lot in dere, ain't it? Let it stay in dere though. Dat ain't nothin'.

Amos: I don' think dat cow ever give dat much milk.

Andy: Yere, grab a-hold o' dat bucket dere an' carry it over dere to de farmhouse.

Amos: Ketch hold of it an' carry half of it, will you?

Andy: My hands is sore. You carry de stuff.

Amos: Whut you goin' do after you give him de milk? We have to go out in de field an' plow, ain't we?

Andy: After I give Mister Hopkins dis yere milk, I'se goin' out in de barn an' take a nap, dat's whut I goin' do.

Amos: Fust thing you know both of us is goin' be fired.

Andy: Whut do we care if we IS fired. Den we kin go to Chicago an' git a big job.

Amos: I know—but we don' wants to lose dis one 'fore we git another one.

Andy: Now lissen, some time when I feel like talkin' to you, I'll tell you how we BOTH kin go up to Chicago an' make a lot o' money.

Amos: De only thing I don' wants to do though—I don' wants to give up one job 'fore I git another one, dat's all.

Andy: Dis job we got now ain't no good. If we git up to Chicago, son, we kin make some big money.

Amos: How is we goin' git dere though, dat's de main thing.

Andy: We'll git dere a'right. Leave it to me. I figures out dem things myself.

Amos: We can't go up dere on no freight train though—we'se li'ble to git killed bummin' our way up dere or sumpin'. We can't do dat.

Andy: Boy, when I leaves dis yere country fur Chicago, I'se goin' fust-class, dat's how I'se goin'.

Amos: I wuz thinkin' dat we might take a couple o' dese yere mules dat dey got down yere—if dey sell 'em cheap enough—drive dem up dere.

Andy: Yere is one man dat ain't goin' out o' yere on no mule. We wouldn't git dere till we was 75 years old.

Amos: Well, yere we is at de house. You goin' give him de milk?

Andy: Han' me de bucket an' den knock on de do'.

Amos: Yere you is. (Knocks on door.)

Andy: I hope dis yere man Hopkins ain't got no mo' work fur me to do today. I'se tired.

Amos: I'se hungry too. Wait a minute—yere he comes.

Hopkins: Alright, boys, you've got the milk, have you?

Andy: Yere you is, Mister Hopkins.

Amos: Dere 'tis right dere.

Hopkins: This is a lot of milk for that cow to be giving.

ANDY: Well, I tell you, Mister Hopkins, I'se been takin' good care o' dat cow an' when I milks 'em, I milks 'em.
HOPKINS: Alright, boys. Now, I want you boys to go over there and fix that barbed wire fence just the other side of the barn. A couple of those posts have fallen down.
ANDY: A'right, Sah, we fix it.
AMOS: Yessah, Mister Hopkins, we take care of it. Come on, Andy.
ANDY: Now lissen yere, I is done enough work 'round dis yere place today.
AMOS: I know, but de man is payin' us by de week. We got do whut he tell us to do.
ANDY: Well, I ain't goin' work MY haid off 'round yere.
AMOS: Well, we GOT fix dat fence. If we don't, we li'ble to git fired.
ANDY: I done tol' you dat we kin go to Chicago an' git a job. Come on, walk in de barn yere wid me.
AMOS: Whut you goin' do in de barn?
ANDY: Don' ast so many questions. Come on in yere wid me like I tell you.
AMOS: We got hurry up an' git out dere on dat fence though.
ANDY: Now lissen yere, son, all we need is de railroad fare to Chicago 'cause dey tells me dat dey is so many jobs open up dere dat dey just can't git 'nuf men to work.
AMOS: Well-a—Whut kind o' job is we goin' git up dere?
ANDY: Well, you ain't got much sense. You can't do nothin' but—well, lemme see—I don' know

WHUT you kin do—but I'se got my job all picked out.

Amos: Whut is YOU goin' do when you git dere?

Andy: I'se goin' be a super-tendent of sumpin'—I goin' be kind of foreman of de job.

Amos: Whut is you gittin' ready to do yere now?

Andy: Come on over yere in de corner yere wid me now.

Amos: Whut is you goin' do yere?

Andy: I'se goin' lay down yere in dis hay an' take a little nap, dat's whut I goin' do.

Amos: Mister Hopkins done told us though to fix dat fence o' his. You can't stay yere—come out yere an' help me.

Andy: You go ahaid and fix de fence. I goin' take a little nap, dat's whut I goin' do.

Amos: 'Spose Mister Hopkins comes out dere though an' wants to know where you is.

Andy: If Mister Hopkins comes out dere an' asts you where I is, tell him one o' his hogs got out de pen an' I is out lookin' fur de hog.

Amos: A'right—I tell him—I'se goin' out an' go to work—I'll see you later.

Andy: Call me when de supper bell rings.

II

Amos and Andy were sent to Atlanta by their employer, Mr. Hopkins, who has a farm just outside Atlanta. Before loading up their wagon with provisions they decided to take a stroll up Decatur Street.

AMOS: Come on Andy, we can't waste too much time. We got git back an' load up dat wagon an' git on back to de farm.
ANDY: Now lissen yere, son, I'se re-gusted wid you. You ain't got no sense. Ev'vy time I try to 'splain sumpin' to you, you don' know whut I'se talkin' 'bout.
AMOS: De trouble wid you is dat you use such big words dat I can't figure 'em out, dat's all.
ANDY: You is thick-haided—dat's de trouble wid you.
AMOS: Well, I tries to understand de best I kin.
ANDY: Well, now come, boy—Let's walk up Decatur Street yere an' look de sights over.
AMOS: I don' guess nothin's goin' happen to dem mules we got tied out in front o' dat store down dere, is dey?
ANDY: If dem mules would run away, dey wouldn't be missed. I tell you dat. Dat's one thing I ain't got no use fur—dat's a lazy mule.

Amos: Tell me dis—you was talkin' 'bout goin' to Chicago. Is Chicago bigger dan Atlanta is?

Andy: Lissen, son—Chicago is a big city. It's so big—well, Chicago—if you would walk from one end o' de town—lemme see yere—Chicago covers mo' miles—well, it's bigger dan dat.

Amos: Chicago's a big town, ain't it?

Andy: To give you a idea o' how big Chicago is, I was talkin' to a fellow dat used to work up dere an' he used to drive a second hand automobile 'round an' he say dat de town is so big dat sometimes when de bridges is up, it take a hour to git from one end o' de town to other.

Amos: Um—um—dat must be some town, ain't it? Whut kind o' bridges is dat you is talkin' 'bout?

Andy: Jest plain bridges, dat's all.

Amos: Whut do de bridges go over?

Andy: Dey go over an' over.

Amos: Dat mus' be some town a'right.

Andy: Not only dat, up in Chicago dey is got— lemme see, how I kin 'splain dis to you.

Amos: 'Splain it to me Andy, 'cause I wants to know 'bout dis yere stuff.

Andy: You is done been in buildin's down yere dat go up in de air.

Amos: Yeah—I done been in some o' dese yere office buildin's in 'em dat has de elevators in 'em.

Andy: Well, dey tell me up in Chicago, dey go sideways.

Amos: Whut you mean, dey go sideways?

Andy: Dis fellow was tellin' me dat when you wants to go from one part o' de town to de other part, to git on de elevator—it take you right dere.

AMOS: Um—um—dat sounds good—I'se gittin' 'thused 'bout dat.

ANDY: Not only dat, dey is got mo' policemens in Chicago dan dey got people.

AMOS: Got mo' policemens up dere, huh? Ain't no chance of us gittin' 'rested if we git up dere, is dey?

ANDY: De policemens up dere means bizness too. Den dey got firemens up dere. Dey must have-a—a hund'ed firemens in dat town.

AMOS: A hund'ed firemens? Um—um.

ANDY: Dat's de thing we wants to do, Amos—We wants to git up dere. Git a big job. Den we kin come down yere an' tell all de boys dat we is big mens an' we is got a lot o' money. Den dey'll think we IS somebody.

AMOS: Dat's a'right—jest so we don't go up dere an' starve to death, dat's all I'se worrin' 'bout.

ANDY: Even if we git up dere an' don't have a job befo' we git dere, we kin find one.

AMOS: Whut you mean, we kin find one?

ANDY: Dey tell me dat de newspapers up dere is full o' want ads, dey is so hard up fur mens to work.

AMOS: Den we ain't goin' have no trouble gittin' a job, is we?

ANDY: All you got do is to pick up a newspaper, find some place dat you like, walk over to see de man an' tell him you is ready to go to work.

AMOS: How 'bout livin' 'spenses? Do it cost a lot?

ANDY: No-no—we kin git a place up dere to live fur little o'nothin'.

AMOS: Dey tells me it's plen'y cold up dere.

ANDY: Well, de cold ain't goin' bother you none.

AMOS: I ought git some warm clothes though 'fore I go up where it's cold. My feets is on de ground now. Look yere at dese shoes o' mine.

ANDY: Boy, we'll make so much money in Chicago de fust week we is dere, dat we kin open up a shoe sto' if we wants to. You know YOU might be thick-haided but I ain't so dumb—I know how to make money.

AMOS: I'se willin' to go up dere a'right. Jest so we know we ain't goin' starve—dat's de main thing.

ANDY: Leave it to me, son. We'll go up dere an' go in bizness.

AMOS: Tell me dis, Andy—somebody was tellin' me dat Chicago was out West—is dat right?

ANDY: Well, if I had a map yere I could show you where 'tis on de map.

AMOS: I heard dat ev'vybody out dere dress up like a cowboy an' dey had buffalos runnin' 'round an' ev'vything.

ANDY: We don' care how dey dress—or we don' care nothin' 'bout de buffalos. De main thing we wants to do is to git up dere an' make some money.

AMOS: You want stop yere in de barber shop yere a minute—see if we see any o' de boys we know?

ANDY: I was goin' in de barber shop anyway to git a haircut.

AMOS: You ain't got no time to git a haircut.

ANDY: Lissen yere, Amos—when I wants to git a haircut I GIT one. Don' try to tell me whut *I* ain't got time to do.

AMOS: We got git back an' load dat wagon up an' git back to de farm, dat's whut we got do.

Andy: Don't worry 'bout dat.
Amos: Look yere—look who's standin' dere in front of de barber shop.
Andy: Well, dere's old Jim.
Amos: Hello dere Jim—how is you?
Jim: Hello boys—whut is you doin' in town?
Andy: Well, I brought Amos in yere, Jim, to git some pur-visions from de market down town yere.
Amos: Yeah—we both come in to git some groceries to take 'em back out to de farm.
Jim: Well, how is ev'vything on de farm, boys?
Andy: Well—it's a'right but we is figgerin' on goin' to Chicago an' git a big job.
Amos: Yeah, dat's whut we is figgerin' on, Jim—we is figgerin' on leavin' yere some time soon an' goin' up to Chicago.
Jim: Well, a lot of de boys goes to de big cities ev'vy now an' den.
Andy: I was jest 'splainin' to Amos yere, Jim, dat a fellow wid my-a—'bility could go up to Chicago dere an' clean up a fortune.
Amos: Whut do you think about it, Jim? You think we kin make any money up dere?
Jim: Well, dat's hard to tell, boys. Some o' de boys from yere went up to New York an' some o' de boys went to Chicago.
Andy: Dey tell me dat Chicago is de place to go fur de big money.
Jim: Two o' de boys dat left yere a month ago wrote one o' de boys back yere a letter de other day—said dat dey wanted to borrow five dollars to git sumpin' to eat wid up dere.
Amos: Dat don' sound so good, do it?

Jim: Another one o' de boys whut went up to Chicago say dat it was so cold up dere one day dat while he was out lookin' fur work both his ears froze up on him.

Amos: Both his ears froze up while he was lookin' fur work, huh?

Andy: He must of looked in de wrong place. I ain't 'spectin' to go up dere an' look out in de snow or nothin'.

Amos: De boy's ears froze up on him, huh?

Jim: An' like a crazy man, dis yere boy poured hot water on his ears—like to ruined him.

Andy: Well, dat man ain't got no sense. De boy was lookin' fur work in de snow.

Amos: Dey tells me, Jim, dat it's mighty cold up dere—is dat right?

Jim: Well, it gits below zero up dere.

Andy: Below zero—dat ain't nothin'.

Amos: Zero sounds bad though—dat sounds like it's cold to me.

Andy: Well—I goin' git on in yere an' git a haircut.

Amos: Wait a minute, Andy—we ain't got no time fur you to git no haircut. We got git back on de farm, you know dat, don't you?

Andy: Now don't gimme no back talk, son. I'se goin' in an' git a haircut.

Amos: Wait a minute yere, Andy—you can't git no haircut now. We got load dat wagon up an' git back out dere, I'm tellin' yo'.

Andy: Jim, do you heah dis thick-haided boy tryin' to tell me whut to do?

Jim: Well, I guess Amos don' want git in no trouble wid de boss.

Amos: Dat's right, Jim—I don' want git in no trouble wid de boss.

Andy: Now lissen—you go on down dere an' load dat wagon up an' den after you git it loaded, drive by yere an' pick me up—by dat time I'll git my haircut.

Amos: A'right den—I'll go on down dere an' load dat wagon up. I wish you'd come on down an' help me though.

Andy: Don' mess wid me son—now go on an' do whut I tell you—ain't I gittin' ready to take you to Chicago?

Amos: Well, I'll go down an' git de wagon loaded up an' come by yere fur you. I'll see you later, Jim.

Jim: Well, so long Amos.

Andy: Wait a minute—you got five cents in yore pocket?

Amos: Yeah, I got five cents.

Andy: Go 'cross de street dere an' git me a seegar—an' bring it over yere 'fore you go down dere.

Amos: A'right, I'll git you one.

III

The boys were walking up Decatur Street in Atlanta when Andy suggested that the two of them flip coins and match for supper. Amos lost and had to pay for both suppers. As we find the two boys now they are on their way to the depot to see if they can get some information about railroad fare to Chicago. Both boys are seriously considering going to the Windy City.

AMOS: Whut is you goin' ast de man when we git down to de depot, Andy—dat's de main thing.

ANDY: Don't make no diff'ence what I ast him, Amos—you jest come on wid me—I 'tends to de bizness.

AMOS: We got git more money dan we got now though to git up dere—I kin tell you dat.

ANDY: Well, maybe dey got some kind o' 'scursion rate up dere. You know, we is got *some* money.

AMOS: I'se done sort of counted on buyin' myself some tan shoes though Sat'day, an' maybe git a new hat or sumpin'.

ANDY: Wait till we git in Chicago an' git yore shoes—dat's de thing to do.

AMOS: De trouble is though—if it's as cold up dere as peoples say it is, my feets is li'ble to freeze up on me.

ANDY: Boy, I'se tellin' you—when we gits up to

Chicago we goin' make so much money dat we goin' be millionaires.

Amos: I certainly would like to have a lot o' money once. If I ever see a hund'ed dollars at one time, I'se li'ble to git married, dat's whut I'se li'ble to do.

Andy: Now listen yere—de fust thing we wants to do is to git up dere in Chicago an' git a good job. Git a good place to live in an' a lot o' stuff to eat.

Amos: Oh yeah—dat's de fust thin' we wants to do a'right. Dat was a pretty good meal we had tonight, wasn't it?

Andy: After we git mo' money though, we kin eat better food dan dat.

Amos: I ain't goin' match you no mo'. Ev'vy time I match you fur sumpin' to eat, I lose an' I have to pay fur both of 'em.

Andy: I'se jest lucky, dat's whut I is.

Amos: I'll say you is lucky. I got save my money if we goin' to Chicago.

Andy: Yere's de depot now—come on, let's git in yere an' talk to dis man an' find out how much it cost to git up dere.

Amos: Dat's a long ways up dere too, ain't it? How long it take us to git up dere?

Andy: Oh, we ought git up dere in two—three days on a fast train.

Amos: Is you goin' up to de window an' talk to de man?

Andy: Yeah—I'll talk to de man. Come on, go up yere wid me though.

Amos: You go ahead, do all de talkin', Andy, 'cause I don' know nothin' 'bout it.

ANDY: Wait a minute 'fore we git up dere now—is you got a pencil so we kin write dis stuff down?
AMOS: I got a little pencil yere if I kin find it. I don' know if it's got no point on it though.
ANDY: See if you can't find de thing. I got have a pencil yere 'cause when I talks to de man, I wants to write down some figures.
AMOS: Yere 'tis, Andy—ain't got much of a point on dere. You might be able to sharpen dat a little bit.
ANDY: Is you got a knife?
AMOS: Hand it to me yere—I'll take my finger nail an' pull some o' dat wood off dere.
ANDY: Don' break de point, now.
AMOS: I ain't goin' break it.
ANDY: Hold on, now—dat's enough.
AMOS: Yere you is, yere you is—go ahaid now.
ANDY: Come on—let's go up to de window yere.
AMOS: I'se wid you—you go ahaid—talk to de man.
ANDY: Mister, kin I ast you a question?
MAN: Sure—what do you want to know?
ANDY: How much do it cost to go from yere to Chicago?
MAN: The fare is $26.72.
ANDY: Dat's twenty-six dollers—an' seventy-two cents. You ain't got nothin' cheaper dan dat, is you?
MAN: No, that's the lowest rate from here to Chicago.
AMOS: Dat's a lot o' money, ain't it?
ANDY: Tell me dis, Mister—if two of us go up dere at one time, will you make it any cheaper?
MAN: No, that will be $26.72 each.
ANDY: Dat means two times dat $26.72, don' it?

Amos: Dat's a lot o' money, Andy.

Andy: Dat's de bes' rate you got, is it?

Man: Yes, that's the best rate. Want a couple of tickets?

Andy: No sah, Mister, don't bother 'bout gittin' us no tickets now—we ain't packed up our things yet. We be back.

Amos: Thank you, Mister—come on Andy, let's git away—figger dis thing out.

Andy: Wait a minute. Say Mister, kin I ast you one mo' question?

Man: Why sure—go ahead—what is it you want?

Andy: You don' charge nothin' extra to carry our baggage up dere, do you?

Man: Oh no. That's included in the $26.72.

Andy: Thank you, Mister.

Amos: Where is you goin' now, Andy?

Andy: I goin' sit down yere. Come on—sit down over yere on dis bench wid me. I wants do some figgerin'.

Amos: Come on—let's sit down yere an' figger dis thing out.

Andy: Now lissen yere—$26.72—dat's whut it cost each one of us.

Amos: Now you is got to times dat by two, ain't you?

Andy: Wait till I do dat yere—twenty-six, seventy-two—times two. Two times two is-a—

Amos: Dat's four.

Andy: No, no—two AN' two is four. We is timesin' yere now.

Amos: Well, two times two is four, ain't it?

Andy: Whut we is got do is to mulsify. You is stackin' 'em up, dat's whut you is doin'. Two

[17]

times two—wait a minute yere now—two times two is six.

Amos: Two times two is six, huh?

Andy: An' nothin' to carry—now-a—two time seven—dere's one right dere.—We is two timesin' $26.72—two times two is six—nothin' to carry—two times seven.

Amos: Dat's two sevens, ain't it?

Andy: Dat can't be seventeen, kin it?

Amos: I know whut dat is. Wait a minute yere—lemme count it on my fingers yere. Dat's fo'teen, ain't it?

Andy: Dat's whut I jest said. Put down a fo' an' carries one. Now, I'll put dat one up yere by dat six. Two times sixteen—

Amos: Whut you goin' do now—mulsify sixteen, huh?

Andy: Well, I got carry dat one—I puts dat one right in between dat two an' de six.

Amos: Whut is we mulsifyin'?

Andy: We'se mulsifyin' $26.72 by two. You see, de fust thing is two times two is six—two times seven is fo'teen—an' I carries one—so dat goes right in between de two an' de six.

Amos: Dat goes right in between de two an' de six, don't it? Put it dere now an' lemme see how it looks.

Andy: Wait a minute yere now—I'll put de one in between de two an' de six—dat makes 216 now.

Amos: Is you goin' mulsify dat 216?

Andy: 'Course I goin' mulsify—whut you think I goin' do wid it.

Amos: Well, whut is dat 216—is dat 216 dollers?

ANDY: You see where I done put dat dot in dere, don't you? Dat makes dat $216.00.
AMOS: Well, when did we git up in dem big figures?
ANDY: Dat's whut happened when you mulsify.
AMOS: Well, go ahaid, do it. You know whut you is doin' dere.
ANDY: Two times 216—lemme see—how much is $216.00 times two?
AMOS: Well, figgerin' it out in my own haid yere, I figures dat dat's over $400.00.
ANDY: I b'lieve you is right... Dat IS right—dat's over $400.00. Two times $26.72, de way I figures yere is over $400.00.
AMOS: Dat certainly is a lot o' money fur us to git up dere on, ain't it?
ANDY: Lissen—I got a idea—we'll fool 'em. I'll go one day an' give $26.72—den de nex' day, don' say nothin' to 'em an' you give $26.72 an' we'll both git dere.
AMOS: Dat's a idea—boy, you certainly do think of 'em.

IV

After drawing their salary the boys start out for Chicago, each having about $35.00 in his pocket. As we find them now they are walking up the road on their way to Atlanta to catch the train for Chicago.

AMOS: I hope you is right about dis yere Chicago thing.
ANDY: Now lissen yere, all you got do is to stick to me when we git up dere an' do whut I tell you to do an' we'll make a lot o' money.
AMOS: De trouble is, you see, de way we is been workin' down yere on dis farm, we had a place to sleep an' plen'y to eat.
ANDY: But de trouble is, we ain't savin' no money. We can't git rich de way we is goin' down yere.
AMOS: I know we can't git rich but it's one thing—we ain't starvin' to death.
ANDY: We got look out fur ourselves—you know dat, don' you?
AMOS: Oh, it ain't no two ways 'bout dat. If we don' look out fur ourselves, it ain't nobody goin' do fur us—I know dat. De only thing, I'se kind of worried 'bout—
ANDY: Now wait a minute—if you is goin' git cold feet 'bout dis yere thing, I ain't goin' take you wid me.

AMOS: I ain't gittin' cold feet 'bout it—I jus' kind of wants to be sho' dat we goin' to git sumpin' to eat up dere—dat's de main thing.
ANDY: We sho' o' gittin' some meat up dere 'cause dat's where de stock yards is.
AMOS: I know, but jest 'cause dey has cows up dere in de stock yards it ain't no sign dat WE kin have some.
ANDY: De thing fur us to do when we git dere is to git a job where we git our meals fur nothin'.
AMOS: Oh, den dat's a'right den—if we kin git de meals fur nothin', dat's a'right.
ANDY: Whut you is got do, is to git mo' 'thused 'bout dis.
AMOS: I'se jest as 'thused as I KIN git.
ANDY: Yere—dis yere suitcase dat I got yere is gittin' heavy. Tote dis fur me a little while.
AMOS: Dis suitcase *I* got is pretty heavy too, you know.
ANDY: Well, you kin kind of balance yore self wid de two o' 'em dere.
AMOS: Dese yere new shoes dat I got too—dey is tight on my feets.
ANDY: Yere, while you is totin' de thing, I'll pull out my pencil yere an' do a little figgerin'.
AMOS: De railroad fare up dere wuz-a—you got it on a piece o' paper dere.
ANDY: Yere 'tis—$26.72.
AMOS: Dat don' 'clude no food on de way up dere, do it?
ANDY: You kin take along a lot o' san'wiches.
AMOS: Whut you goin' take?
ANDY: I ain't goin' eat nothin' 'less I git hungry or

sumpin' an' den I'll take a couple bites o' whut you got.

AMOS: You better take along sumpin', 'cause I don' want spen' all my money fur san'wiches 'fore I git up dere.

ANDY: You know, on de way up dere on de train, I'se got do a lot o' figgerin'.

AMOS: Whut is you goin' figger?

ANDY: I got figger whut kind o' job I wants an' whut kind o' job I got git you. Lemme see yere —you kin do de heavy work 'cause you ain't got much sense as I is.

AMOS: Well, whut kind o' work is you figgerin' on fur yore self?

ANDY: I'se done come to de 'clusion dat I'se goin' be a manager o' sumpin'.

AMOS: You mean, up in Chicago, you goin' be a manager?

ANDY: Dat's de kind o' job I goin' git myself.

AMOS: You can't git me none like dat, kin you?

ANDY: Well, you is got quan-tify fur a job like dat.

AMOS: How kin you quan-tify?

ANDY: You is got show de mens up dere dat you is de man dey is lookin' fur.

AMOS: How do I know who dey is lookin' fur though?

ANDY: Dat's jest it.

AMOS: Oh.

ANDY: You see, I know de mens dey is lookin' fur.

AMOS: Whut mens *is* dey lookin' fur? How come dey is lookin' fur 'em?

ANDY: Dey is always lookin' fur mens.

AMOS: Whut's de matter—is dese mens been runnin' away or sumpin'?

ANDY: Don' git me mad now—don' git me mad.
AMOS: I jest didn't know—I jest wanted you to 'splain it to me, dat's all. I certainly wish you'd tote dese two suitcases fur me fur a minute though—I'se gittin' tired.
ANDY: Now, if you goin' start hollerin' 'bout gittin' tired 'fore you do some work, I ain't goin' take you wid me.
AMOS: I don' mean to be hollerin' but dese yere things is heavy. You got a lot o' tools in yore suitcase.
ANDY: I tell you whut you do—you tote de two suitcases to de train an' I'll take care of 'em all de way to Chicago.
AMOS: Whut you mean—you want me to tote 'em to de train—den you goin' take 'em, huh?
ANDY: We ain't got but one mo' mile an' a half to go. Dat's all YOU got tote de things. Den I'll take 'em all de way to Chicago—dat's fair enough, ain't it?
AMOS: Oh yeah—dat's fair enough.
ANDY: Now, lissen yere—I wuz jest thinkin' 'bout sumpin'.
AMOS: I got set dese things down an' rest a minute—dat's whut I got do.
ANDY: Go ahaid—sit 'em down fur a minute dere.
AMOS: Lemme sit down on one of 'em yere. Go ahaid, talk to me now—my back hurts me.
ANDY: Yere, wait a minute. YOU sit on dis one—let ME sit on dat one.
AMOS: Dere you is—now go ahaid, tell me whut you goin' tell me.
ANDY: When we gits up to Chicago, you leave ev'vything to me.

Amos: Whut you mean, leave it to you—'bout eatin'?

Andy: I ain't talkin' 'bout eatin'—I'se talkin' 'bout bizness now.

Amos: Oh, I goin' leave it to you a'right. I goin' do jest whut you tell me to do.

Andy: In case a man offers us a job soon as we git in town, 'tain't no use to grab de fust one you sees—let's look 'round.

Amos: Oh, no—we wants to look 'round a'right—but on de other hand-a—we got make some money kind of quick, ain't we?

Andy: Now-a—let's 'magine now dat we is sittin' in a man's office.

Amos: Whut man's office?

Andy: A man up in Chicago's office.

Amos: We ain't up in Chicago—we is sittin' down yere on de road on two suitcases, dat's whut we is doin'.

Andy: No, no, now lissen—don' git me mad—don' git me mad—play like you is in a man's office in Chicago.

Amos: We ain't got no time to be playin' yere, Andy—we got git over to de depot.

Andy: I'se gonna show you though how to act when we git in de man's office. Now, yere we is sittin' in de man's office.

Amos: I don' see no office but go ahaid.

Andy: Whut is de fust thing you goin' say to de man?

Amos: I ast him fur a job—dat's de fust thing.

Andy: No, no, I mean when you fust walk in de office—whut is de fust thing you goin' say?

Amos: I'll say "hello."

ANDY: 'Tain't no use to try to git nothin' in yore haid, boy. Now, lissen to me—yere we is in de man's office—de man han' each one of us a seegar. By de way, keep de seegars dey give you up dere—you don' smoke 'em so give 'em to me when we git out.
AMOS: De trouble is though—we can't live on seegars—de mans got give us mo' dan dat.
ANDY: Now, yere we is sittin' in de man's office. De gent'man says—I have two jobs open—one at a hund'ed dollers a week an' another one at seventy-five dollers a week. Kin you-a—mens go to work right away? Whut is you goin' tell him?
AMOS: I'd say—tell me where de jobs is Mister—I'll run all de way over dere.
ANDY: Dat's where you is wrong.
AMOS: Whut would YOU tell him?
ANDY: De fust thing I'd say to him—I'd say—hold on yere, Mister—we can't work fur no cheap money like dat.
AMOS: No CHEAP money? Dat's big money, ain't it?
ANDY: Dat's pin money up dere. I'd ast him—I'd say—is dat by de day or by de week?
AMOS: Um—um—dat certainly is a lot o' money, ain't it?
ANDY: Hund'ed dollers a week de man offers us.
AMOS: Whut man is dat?
ANDY: De man in Chicago.
AMOS: Is you got his address?
ANDY: Yere we is in his office—sittin' right yere in de man's office now an' he done offered us a hund'ed dollers a week.

AMOS: He's done offered us a hund'ed dollers a week, is he?

ANDY: Now whut is de nex' thing to tell de man?

AMOS: Ast him when we kin go to work.

ANDY: No, no, dat's where yore wrong.

AMOS: Whut is de nex' thing to tell him?

ANDY: I leans back in my chair, puts my feets up on his desk, knocks de ashes off my seegar like dis—an' says-a—I'se sorry Mister but we can't take de job.

AMOS: Um—um—you goin' tell de man dat, huh? Turn down a hund'ed dollers a week.

ANDY: Boy, dat is pin money—pick up dem suitcases an' come on yere. You follows me an' you'll be a millionaire.

AMOS: I be doggone—we goin' to Chicago an' make a lot o' money—come on, let's git goin' yere.

V

Just before boarding the train for Chicago Amos and Andy met a friend who gave them some very bad news. Although Amos is a little afraid to leave Atlanta, Andy has convinced him of the possibilities in Chicago for energetic men. We find the boys now on a train Chicago-bound.

Amos: De only trouble wid dis yere thing, Andy, I didn't lak whut dat fellow tol' us jest 'fore we got on de train.
Andy: You ain't goin' pay no 'tention to ever'thing you heah, is you? I tell you I know whut I'se doin'.
Amos: I ain't 'sputin' yore word. De only thing I'se thinkin' 'bout is gittin' sumpin' to eat when we git up dere 'cause after buyin' dese yere san'wiches, I ain't got but eight dollers.
Andy: Dat ain't nothin' to be 'fraid of. I ain't got but thirteen dollers myself.
Amos: 'Spose we git in Chicago dere an' we can't find work right away—dis yere money ain't goin' last us long, is it?
Andy: Lissen yere—when we gits to Chicago, de minute we step off de train, dey is li'ble to come right up to us an' grab us.
Amos: Grab us fur whut? Put us in jail or sumpin'?
Andy: No, no—grab us an' ask us if we want a job.

Amos: You heard whut John tol' us though back dere at de depot, ain't you?

Andy: Whut you mean—about dem two boys goin' to Chicago?

Amos: Yeah—he say dem boys went up dere an' starved to death.

Andy: De trouble wid dem boys is—both of 'em was like you. Dey didn't have no sense—but wid a man like me along dat knows how to handle big bizness mens, we ain't goin' have no trouble.

Amos: I goin' let you do all de talkin' when we git up dere. You git de jobs and I'll do my share o' de work.

Andy: I done tol' you dat I'se goin' git myself a job managin' sumpin'.

Amos: If I kin manage to git a job, I'll be a'right.

Andy: No, better han' me one o' dem san'wiches o' yours dere.

Amos: You didn't bring none, did you?

Andy: No, I'se been busy figgerin' out whut we goin' do. I ain't had no time to buy san'wiches.

Amos: Whut kind you want—you wants a cheese san'wich or a ham san'wich?

Andy: Whut kind you got?

Amos: I got two ham san'wiches an' two cheese san'wiches.

Andy: I'll eat de two ham san'wiches.

Amos: You goin' eat both of 'em?

Andy: Dat's whut I goin' do—I got have some meat in me.

Amos: I'd lak to have some meat in me too. I'd lak to have ONE o' dem ham san'wiches.

Andy: Lissen yere, Amos—de man dat does de haid

work is got build up his body—an' I can't do nothin' wid cheese.

AMOS: Dat's a'right, Andy—I'll eat de cheese den 'cause you goin' take care of ever'thing, ain't you?

ANDY: Gimme dem two ham san'wiches. Is you got any coffee?

AMOS: No, I ain't got no coffee.

ANDY: You don' mean to tell me dat you came 'way from Atlanta widout some coffee to drink on de train?

AMOS: I ain't brought no coffee.

ANDY: Boy, you never thinks o' nothin'. YOU know I got have coffee when I eats san'wiches.

AMOS: How come *you* didn't bring no coffee?

ANDY: How is I goin' bring coffee when I'se tryin' to figger up ever'thing—keep my money straight, think about Chicago an' ever'thing else.

AMOS: Go ahaid—eat dat ham san'wich den.

ANDY: Well—yere goes de san'wich.

AMOS: How do it taste?

ANDY: (with mouth full of sandwich) Lissen yere—de nex' time you order ham san'wiches put some mustard on de things.

AMOS: I don' b'lieve I'll eat my cheese san'wiches right now. I ain't crazy 'bout cheese.

ANDY: How come you buy cheese if you ain't crazy 'bout it?

AMOS: Well, de ham san'wiches cost ten cents an' de cheese cost five cents—so I thought I'd get two cheese san'wiches.

ANDY: Move dat suitcase dere so I kin put my feets up over dere, will you?

AMOS: You ain't figgerin' on goin' to sleep, is you?
ANDY: After I finish eatin' yere, I goin' take a little nap. Kind of un-lax myself.
AMOS: Dis yere train is certainly goin', you know it?
ANDY: Boy, we is headin' fur Chicago now.
AMOS: Look out dere at all de farms an' ever'thing —you know I kind of hates to leave dis yere part o' de country.
ANDY: Don't git cold feet now. Nothin' gits me mo' re-gusted dan to have somebody wid me wid cold feet.
AMOS: I ain't gittin' cold feet. I'se jest tninkin' dat we ain't got no friends up dere. Might be a good idea to kind of hold on to whut little money we got till we git sumpin' to do.
ANDY: Now lissen yere, Amos—de trouble wid you is, you can't re'lize de 'portance of gittin' to de destitution.
AMOS: I ain't re'lized none o' dat stuff yet.
ANDY: Is you got dat little pencil wid you? I'll show you some figgerin' dat will make you wish you'd gone to Chicago years ago.
AMOS: Yere's de little pencil, Andy.
ANDY: Now, gimme a piece o' paper.
AMOS: Yere you is—yere's a little piece o' paper.
ANDY: How much money do you wants to make?
AMOS: I wants to make all I KIN make.
ANDY: Well now, lissen yere, you got help me wid dis thing. You got give me some figger to start wid. Name a big figger.
AMOS: Well—say a thousan' dollers—dat's whut I'd like to make—a thousan' dollers.
ANDY: A'right—I'll show you how to make it.

AMOS: Go ahaid—'splain it to me how I goin' make it.
ANDY: Now, de fust thing you do—you gits to Chicago.
AMOS: Wid eight dollers.
ANDY: Well, now, dere you is right dere.
AMOS: Dere I is right where?
ANDY: Right dere wid eight dollers. Now den—you starts figgerin'.
AMOS: Figgerin' how I goin' keep from starvin' to death?
ANDY: Now, wait a minute—don't git me re-gusted.
AMOS: Well, go ahaid, 'splain it to me.
ANDY: You is got eight dollers an' you is in Chicago.
AMOS: An' I ain't had nothin' to eat—dat's goin' take some o' de eight.
ANDY: Whut you wants to make is a thousan' dollers, ain't it?—an' you got eight dollers. Now, lemme see.
AMOS: Dat's whut I wants to do—make a thousan' dollers an' I ain't got but eight.
ANDY: De fust thing you got do, you got take yore money to de bank an' have it compounded.
AMOS: Whut you mean—I take de eight dollers down to de bank an' ast 'em to compound it, huh?
ANDY: You gives yore money to de bank an' tell 'em to semi-annual compound it fur you. Right dere is where yore money starts figgerin' up.
AMOS: Well, whut do I do while de bank is got de eight dollers, eyein' it an' 'poundin' it?
ANDY: Dat's when yore money is workin' fur you.
AMOS: Whut good is it goin' do me if de bank is got it?

ANDY: You don' 'speck de bank to compound de money while you got it, do you?

AMOS: Can't I kind of stand in de bank dere while dey is doin' dat to it an' watch 'em do it—an' den when dey finishes, I kin take it away wid me.

ANDY: No, no-Amos—whut de bank is goin' do is to double yore money.

AMOS: How long is dat goin' take though?

ANDY: Till de intrest climbs up.

AMOS: Up where?

ANDY: Up to where one doller equals two dollers.

AMOS: Well, how do I git de thousan' dollers though—dat's whut I'se figgerin' 'bout.

ANDY: De minute you git dere, you start 'vestin' yore money.

AMOS: Whut you mean 'vestin' it?

ANDY: Put it *in* sumpin'.

AMOS: I'll put it in my shoe.

ANDY: No, no—don' git me mad now—don' git me mad.

AMOS: Whut you mean, 'vest it den?

ANDY: You wants to buy sumpin' dat will do you some good.

AMOS: Den I'll git myself some ham an' eggs.

ANDY: 'Tain't no use fur me to try to 'splain nothin' to you, Amos—I'se tryin' to 'lighten you an' you won't be lit.

AMOS: Well, anyway, I got eight dollers, ain't I?

ANDY: You KNOW you got dat. Now den, you wants a thousan'—all you is got git is de diff'ence between dat eight dollers an' de thousan'—den you is got it.

AMOS: Dat's whut I got do, ain't it?

CONDUCTOR: Chattanooga next stop—Chattanooga, Tennessee.
AMOS: Whut's dis town we'se comin' into now—Chattanoogey?
ANDY: Dat's whut de train is stoppin' fur. Dis next town is Chattanoogey.
AMOS: Chattanoogey Tennessee—Um—um.
ANDY: Wait a minute yere, Amos—Where is you goin'?
AMOS: When de train stops yere I is jest goin' step off yere fur a second in Chattanoogey.
ANDY: Whut you want do—stretch yore legs?
AMOS: No, I jest wants to git my feet in Dixie once mo'—dat's all.
ANDY: Wait a minute—I'll go wid you—come on, let's go.

VI

Amos and Andy arrived in the Windy City and after talking to a policeman regarding work Amos became very discouraged. As we find the boys now, they are in the depot seated on one of the benches, a little undecided just what to do.

AMOS: De way dat policeman talk, Andy, I kind of got un'couraged.
ANDY: Don' pay no 'tention to whut de peoples say to you up yere. We gits a job a'right.
AMOS: You tol' me though 'fore I left Atlanta dat peoples would meet us at de depot yere wantin' to give us a job.
ANDY: Lissen, Amos—we goin' git a job yere—now don' worry.
AMOS: We BETTER git one 'cause we is certainly a long ways from home, I tell you dat.
ANDY: Don' worry—I'll take care o' you on de job —even if I have to git you a job an' be yore manager.
AMOS: I'se willin' to do anything 'cause I ain't got but $7.50.
ANDY: Now, whut kind o' work do you wants to do?
AMOS: Any kind o' work—jest so I kin work an' make some money—dat's whut I wants to do.

ANDY: Do you wants to do brain work or back work?

AMOS: I better start out doin' some hard work, I guess, 'cause I don' know much about dis yere Chicago.

ANDY: Lemme think yere a minute.

AMOS: Is we goin' sit in de depot yere all de time?

ANDY: Well, if we *don't* sit yere, where is we goin'?

AMOS: Go out an' git a job.

ANDY: You ain't ready to go to work now—dressed all up dere like you is.

AMOS: If a man gimme a job though, all I got do is take off my coat an' go to work.

ANDY: De way I figgers de thing out, de thing fur you to do is fur *you* to git a job till *I* kin git fixed 'round.

AMOS: Whut you mean?—'splain dat to me.

ANDY: Well, now yere's de thing—it ain't no use fur a man like me to go out an' take de fust job I run across.

AMOS: No, no, I don' want you to do nothin' dat you don' wants to do—but on de other hand, we is got eat, ain't we?

ANDY: Dat's whut I say-a—we kin git a room somewhere an' YOU kin git a job. Den de money dat YOU bring home we kin live on till I kin git de kind o' job I wants.

AMOS: Whut is you goin' be doin' though while I'se workin'?

ANDY: Somebody's got stay at home 'case some man sends after us.

AMOS: Whut you goin' do—wait at home till somebody sends fur you, huh?

ANDY: Dat's de idea.

Amos: But you goin' git me a job 'fore you do dat, ain't you?

Andy: Dat's right—you see, Amos—I ain't like de ever'day man dat you runs into—I looks ahaid—I got ever'thing figgered out fur you. Pretty soft fur you bein' yere wid me.

Amos: Well, how long is we goin' sit yere in de depot—dat's de nex' thing I wants to know 'bout.

Andy: We is jest as good yere as we is anywhere else.

Amos: Whut you mean, we'se jest as good yere?

Andy: Ain't no tellin' when a man is li'ble to run up yere to us an' offer us a couple hund'ed dollers a week or sumpin'.

Amos: We better stay yere all night den, 'cause if a man ever offer me dat much an' tells me de job is mine I'm goin' to some res'trant an' git myself four dollers worth o' ham an' eggs.

Andy: We is sittin' right yere in de spotlight. (surprised) Oh!

Amos: Whut's de matter, whut's de matter?

Andy: Did you see dat man dat jest passed yere?

Amos: You mean dat man goin' down dere?

Andy: Dat's de one—I thought *sho'* dat man was comin' over yere an' offer us two hund'ed dollers a week.

Amos: He ain't said nothin' though when he passed, did he?

Andy: Maybe he didn't see us.

Amos: We can't sit yere in de depot all de time though, kin we?

Andy: Whut's de use o' goin' out on de street an' git run over by a automobile out dere?

Amos: I'se hungry, I is.
Andy: Now lemme git to figgerin' yere.
Amos: Whut is you goin' figger?
Andy: How I kin git you a job. Now-a—How much is you willin' to start out on?
Amos: I'll start out on anything—jest so I git a job.
Andy: Let's see how much we need to live on.
Amos: You goin' live on whut *I* make, is you?
Andy: Till I git started.
Amos: When is you plannin' on gittin' started?
Andy: I don' wants to make a mistake when I starts out—I wants to git de right job at fust so I ain't got keep changin' 'round.
Amos: No, no, I wants you to git de right job a' right.
Andy: In case we can't git you no job in de nex' few minutes—dat is, de kind o' job dat you ought to have—I might find you a job washin' dishes in some res'trant—den we is sho' o' sumpin' to eat.
Amos: Well, we got pay room rent, you know dat, don' you?
Andy: Well, we'll find some money 'round somewheres.
Amos: You tol' me though dat soon as we got yere in Chicago dat ever'body would grab us.
Andy: Dat's whut I'se waitin' yere fur.
Amos: Well, let's git out in de street so people kin see us.
Andy: Now, wait a minute—lemme figger—lend me dat pencil again.
Amos: Yere you is—Yere's de pencil.
Andy: 'Case anybody comes by yere an' see us now

—see me figgerin' yere, dey'll KNOW dat I'se a man dat knows how to figger. I better carry a pencil wid me all de time.

AMOS: You better git a longer one dan dat though 'cause dey can't see dat one.

ANDY: Now lemme see—today is whut?

AMOS: Today is Monday.

ANDY: M-o-n-d-a-y—Monday.

AMOS: Whut is you figgerin'?

ANDY: Shut up.

AMOS: Well, whut is you figgerin' dere—'splain it to me.

ANDY: Monday, Tuesday, Wed., Thurs., Fri., Sat'day—dere's six workin' days.

AMOS: Dat's right—dat's six workin' days.

ANDY: Well, dere you is.

AMOS: Dere I is whut?

ANDY: Now you know whut days you has to work.

AMOS: I know de days a'right—de place is de thing I'se worried 'bout.

ANDY: Well, come on, let's git out o' yere so peoples kin see us. Pick up dem suitcases.

AMOS: Dese yere things certainly is heavy.

ANDY: You must of put a lot o' crow-bars in yore suitcase or sumpin', didn't you?

AMOS: I got my new shoes in dere. Dey kind of weights it down some.

ANDY: Well, let's git on out in de street yere now.

AMOS: Whut is all dem automobiles—taxicabs?

ANDY: Looks like dey is havin' a taxicab parade yere.

AMOS: Ain't no use fur us to git in none o' dem things. Dey EATS up money.

ANDY: De fust thing I got do is git you a job.

Amos: I know a boy up yere.
Andy: Who you know up yere?
Amos: You 'member old David from Atlanta? He's up yere somewheres.
Andy: You don' know where he is though—you'll never find him up yere. Dey got 15 or 20 thousan' peoples in dis town.
Amos: Looks like dey got dat many taxicabs yere to me. I got set down dese yere suitcases—dey is heavy.
Andy: I wonder which way we better go?
Amos: I don' know—dat's up to you. I'll go anywhere you say go.
Andy: Wait a minute—yere come a man now—he goin' give us a job—look out.
Amos: You talk to him.
Andy: Keep quiet now—lemme do de talkin'.
Man: Say, buddy, will you lemme have two bits to git a cup o' coffee an' something to eat?
Andy: Amos takes care o' all dis kind o' stuff. Amos, give de man two bits.
Amos: Whut you want—two bits, Mister?
Man: Yeah, I'm pretty hungry—I been out o' work for six months. Can't find a job.
Amos: Yere you is, Mister—yere's two bits.
Man: Much obliged, Buddy.
Andy: Come on now, let's go.
Amos: Andy—is you sho' dey needs mens up yere?
Andy: Come on now—don' git me mad—don' git me mad.

VII

Amos and Andy decided to find some place to get a room. They tried one rooming house but became frightened and left. We find the two boys now on the South Side of Chicago standing on a corner—Amos is carrying his suitcase and Andy's suitcase.

AMOS: Lissen yere, Andy, we got git *some* place, dat's one thing we GOT do.
ANDY: Don' rush me now—don' rush me, Amos.
AMOS: I ain't rushin' you but dese yere suitcases is gittin' heavy. I wish you'd carry one o' dese.
ANDY: Now lissen, we got figger out where we goin' stay yere—dat's one thing we GOT do.
AMOS: I didn't lak dat las' place we looked at.
ANDY: When we heard dem two mens talkin' in de room, son, dat's when I sold out.
AMOS: Dis yere certainly is a big town, ain't it?
ANDY: Dat's whut I tol' you—we could come up yere an' git in a big city like Chicago an' make a lot o' money.
AMOS: Dey certainly is a mess o' peoples yere. Look at all de peoples.
ANDY: Dat's whut I been tryin' to 'splain to you, Amos. Wid all dese people up yere dey needs men to work.
AMOS: You tol' me though dat soon as we got yere

somebody wuz goin' grab us an' give us a big job.
ANDY: Well, dat's right.
AMOS: Ain't nobody grabbed us yet though.
ANDY: De trouble is—you totin' dese suitcases up de street yere, ever'body thinks you is already workin'.
AMOS: How come dey don't grab you an' give *you* a job?
ANDY: Dey thinks I'se helpin' you.
AMOS: Dey is certainly wrong dere. I wish you WOULD help me—dese things is heavy.
ANDY: Don' git me mad now—don' git me mad.
AMOS: Well, whut is we goin' do now—dat's de main thing.
ANDY: Let's walk up de street yere an' see if we kin run into anybody dat will give us a job.
AMOS: Dat's whut we BEEN doin'—we walked all de way up yere from de depot an' dey ain't nobody said nothin' to us.
ANDY: Don't git dis-recouraged now. Stone heart never won fair lady.
AMOS: I ain't got no stone heart but my feets hurt me an' my hands start hurtin' me now from totin' dese yere things.
ANDY: We ought to git a room de fust thing so I kin sit down.
AMOS: If we DON'T git one pretty soon, I'se goin' fall down.
ANDY: We don't need no whole house—all we need is one room.
AMOS: I'd be satisfied if I could jest git a corner of a room. I'se so tired I could sleep standin' up right now.

ANDY: Well, let's walk up yere one mo' block—maybe somebody'll grab us in dis block an' give us a job.
AMOS: Whut street is dis we're on now?
ANDY: Yere's a sign up yere on de corner—wait a minute, I'll read it to you.
AMOS: Whut do it say?
ANDY: Dis yere is State Street an' 35th Street.
AMOS: Dat don' mean nothin' to me.
ANDY: Whut street is you LOOKIN' fur?
AMOS: I ain't lookin' fur *no* street. I kind of wish though dat I wuz standin' on Peachtree Street in Atlanta though—dat's whut I wish.
ANDY: Don't git cold feets now, Amos.
AMOS: My feets is already cold.
ANDY: De thing WE got do is git a room, an' den git a job.
AMOS: Don't look like we goin' do neither one of 'em to me.
ANDY: How kin I do wid you walkin' along yere complainin' 'bout ever'thing? You is in Chicago, ain't you?
AMOS: Yeah—we is yere in Chicago but don't nobody know 'bout it.
ANDY: Maybe we ought to have our pitchers put in de paper or sumpin' so dey'll know we is yere.
AMOS: It's a lot o' fellows walkin' 'round de street yere—don't look lak dey is workin' to me.
ANDY: Sit dem suitcases down over yere. Lemme figger wid you.
AMOS: Dat's de bes' thing you done say—sit dese things down. Look at my hands yere—dey is

got cal-looses on 'em yere from carryin' dem things.

ANDY: How much money is you got?

AMOS: I'se got $6.80—dat's whut I got left.

ANDY: It's almost time fur us to eat again.

AMOS: I'se goin' git me five hot dogs fur supper.

ANDY: I wants to git some po'k chops, dat's whut I wants to git.

AMOS: Well, whut is we goin' do—we can't sit yere on de corner all de time.

ANDY: Well, if you wants to, you got $6.80—we kin take a couple o' dollers o' dat an' git a automobile fur 'bout half a hour an' look de town over.

AMOS: I don' wants to see de town. I wants to git a room, dat's whut I wants to do—den I wants to git a job.

ANDY: Now, lemme figger yere. Dis yere is Chicago.

AMOS: Yeah—Yere we is sittin' on State Street in Chicago.

ANDY: Dey ain't but one thing fur you to do, Amos.

AMOS: Whut's dat, Andy?

ANDY: I better take you down to de 'ployment agency.

AMOS: Whut you mean, you goin' take ME down dere? Ain't YOU goin' down dere too?

ANDY: One o' de fust things I wants to do is git YOU to work so you'll be happy and satisfied.

AMOS: How come you don't git yore self a job at one o' dese yere 'ployment agencies?

ANDY: Now, yere's de thing. Dey needs men like us to work up yere an' when we walk in dere dey

[43]

might wants to put us to work before we gits supper.

AMOS: I wish somebody WOULD gim*me* a job.

ANDY: Pick up dese yere suitcases now an' let's git down de street an' see if we kin find a 'ployment agency.

AMOS: I'se gittin' plenty hungry, I know dat.

ANDY: Maybe we ought to git a room befo' we go to de 'ployment agency.

AMOS: Dat WOULD be de best thing to do, I b'lieve. Den I kin set dese yere suitcases down.

ANDY: I kin sit down an' un-lax myself.

AMOS: De main thing is now to find out where we goin' git dis yere room, ain't it?

ANDY: We ought to be able to git a room fur 'bout fo' dollers or five dollers a week. If we paid five dollers, you got $6.80—dat would leave you $1.80 de way I figgers.

AMOS: Well, whut is I got do, pay fur de room?

ANDY: You 'vance de money an' I'll talk bizness. Den you 'members whut you done spent. Den when de money starts comin' in, I'll re-burse you.

AMOS: Whut you goin' do to me?

ANDY: Whut did I say I wuz goin' do?

AMOS: You say I wuz to spend de money an' den when de money come in you wuz goin' re-burse me.

ANDY: Did I say re-burse? If I did dat was a typewriter error—dat should be un-re-burse. Dat's whut I'll do fur you.

AMOS: I don' know whut you say but you do it anyway.

ANDY: Now, de fust thing we ought to do is to git a room near our job.
AMOS: How we goin' do dat?—we ain't got no job.
ANDY: Well, den we ought to git a job near de room den.
AMOS: Whut you mean, live near where we is workin', huh?
ANDY: We ought to live near where YOU is workin' fur de fust two weeks 'cause maybe you'll have to git to work earlier.
AMOS: Whut time is YOU plannin' on gittin' to work?
ANDY: Well, don' worry 'bout me—I got git you settled first.
AMOS: Well, I goin' set dese suitcases down yere till you make up yore mind which way we is goin'.
ANDY: Lend me dat pencil a minute yere.
AMOS: Yere you is—whut you goin' figger now?
ANDY: One an' one is two—two an' two is fo'—
AMOS: De fust thing you know we goin' be yere in Chicago flat broke.
ANDY: Whut you mean, flat broke?
AMOS: We goin' be hungry an' we ain't goin' have no money to eat wid.
ANDY: Ain't I figgerin' right yere now? Whut you think I'se doin' wid dis pencil?—Well, de anser is—we got git a room now.
AMOS: We better git one top o' some res'trant or sumpin'. Den if we ain't got no money, dem fumes dat comes up from de kitchen might help us some.
ANDY: Well, come on den—let's see if we can't git a room—pick up dem suitcases.
AMOS: Come on den—Let's go.

VIII

Amos and Andy finally succeeded in getting a room on the South Side and while glancing through the afternoon paper, Amos saw an ad which sounded pretty good. The boys decided to call the advertiser on the telephone and as we find them now Amos is standing in the hall of the boarding house by the telephone with the receiver to his ear while Andy brings up a chair and is seated by Amos ready to offer his suggestions.

AMOS: De people don't answer yere, Andy—whut mus' I do?
ANDY: Shake de hook a couple times dere.
AMOS: Look yere—my nickel done come back to me. I be doggoned—de nickel done come right back.
ANDY: Dat's de crazies' thing I done ever heard of. Put de nickel in again an' start over. Ast de telephone lady dere whut's de trouble wid her.
AMOS: Yere goes de nickel.
ANDY: Ast her how come you git de nickel back.
AMOS: Wait a minute—yere she is. Hello lady—I jest called a number an' you gimme my nickel back—whut you do dat fur?—de line must of been busy, huh?—whut's dat?—hol' de 'phone a minute—lemme find out yere. (To Andy) De lady wants to know whut number I called —she say she try to git it fur me.

ANDY: *You* is de one dat called de number—I don' know whut de number wuz.
AMOS: Wait a minute lady—I got find de number again—I done lost it. Don't lose my nickel.
ANDY: Lookit yere—dere de nickel come back again—dat's de crazies' telephone I done ever seed.
AMOS: Whut wuz de number I called? It's on dat piece o' paper dere.
ANDY: Dat was de number dat you got out o' de want ad section of de afte'noon paper, ain't it?
AMOS: Dat was dat advertisement dat I done read in de paper—call Superior 0030.
ANDY: Now, wait a minute 'fore you call dat number. Whut do de advertisement say?
AMOS: Yere 'tis, right yere. Read it to me—whut DO it say?
ANDY: It say yere—'Wanted one man fur outside work—good pay, steady 'ployment.'
AMOS: 'Steady 'ployment' huh?—Um—um.
ANDY: Now, you knows what dat means, don' you?
AMOS: 'Splain it to me—whut DO dat mean?
ANDY: Dat mean dat's a—if you gits de job, WE don' have to worry 'bout a place to sleep and sumpin' to eat fur a few weeks.
AMOS: Whut you mean,—we-we-WE ain't goin' worry? Ain't you goin' git sumpin' to do? Ain't you goin' start worryin'?
ANDY: Now lissen yere, Amos—dere's all kind o' men in dis world an' I'se one o' de kind dat can't stand no worry.
AMOS: Whut you mean, you can't stand no worry?
ANDY: If I start worryin' 'bout a job fur myself I'se li'ble to git sick from worry an' de fust thing I know I'll be in bed.

AMOS: How you goin' git a job if you don't start thinkin' 'bout one?

ANDY: De thing to do is to git YOU a job fust. Den I kin kind of look after you—den if sumpin' GOOD come up, I'll take it.

AMOS: Well, whut mus' I do—call up dis yere man?

ANDY: Call him up again now. Now when you git him—now wait a minute—lemme tell you.

AMOS: Go ahaid—I'se listenin'.

ANDY: When you git de man on de telephone, be in-rependent—don't let him think dat you WANT de job.

AMOS: But I DO want it—I ain't got no money hardly.

ANDY: Wait a minute yere—don't let de man *know* dat you is hard up.

AMOS: Whut mus' I tell de man den?

ANDY: Let de man think dat you is doin' him a favor to go to work fur him.

AMOS: Let him think dat I'se doin' him a favor to go to work fur him, huh?

ANDY: Dat's de way. Now, go ahaid, call him. De number is SUPerior 0030.

AMOS: Yere goes dat nickel again. Hello—I want Superior 0030—yes ma'am, dat's de number.

ANDY: Don't furgit now. Talk up to de man—let him think you is SOMEBODY.

AMOS: Who mus' I make him think I is?

ANDY: Make him think you is a big man dat ain't crazy fur work.

AMOS: Wait a minute—hello—is dis yere Superior 0030?—dis yere's Amos—I say, dis yere's Amos—Dis yere is Amos Jones—

ANDY: Tell him I'se yere wid you too.

Amos: Hello—Andy is yere too—I say Andy Brown is yere wid me too—my name is-a—Amos—
Andy: Tell him you ain't crazy 'bout de job.
Amos: I ain't crazy 'bout de job—Whut's dat?—I say I ain't crazy 'bout de job—Whut's dat? —Hold de phone a minute—(To Andy) Andy, he says whut job?
Andy: Tell him de job dat he had in de paper.
Amos: Hello—De job dat you done had in de paper—no, no, I done seed de thing in de paper—say call you up—You want a man fur outside work—a'right say, do dat.
Andy: Whut he say?
Amos: He say dat he goin' git de man on de telephone dat handles dat stuff.
Andy: Now, wait a minute—
Amos: I can't wait long—he's goin' git de man right now—whut you wants to tell me?
Andy: Ast de man how much de job pay an' no matter whut he tell you, tell him dat ain't enough.
Amos: Whut you mean, tell him dat ain't enough?
Andy: Now lissen, dat's whut you call sy-rology.
Amos: Dat's whut you call whut?
Andy: If de man tell you de job pay fifty dollers a week, tell him dat ain't enough—dat's sy-rology.
Amos: Whut in de world is sy-rology?
Andy: Sy-rology is when you start eatin' on a man's brain.
Amos: Wait a minute—wait a minute—hello—dis yere's Amos talkin'—I say dis yere's Amos—My name is Amos Jones—Hold de phone a minute (to Andy)

[49]

ANDY: Whut's de matter now?
AMOS: He say whut kin I do fur you?
ANDY: Tell him you wants to talk to him.
AMOS: Hello Mister—Dis yere's Amos again—I wants to talk to you—whut's dat?—I don't know whut I want but I wants to talk to you though—dis yere's Amos—
ANDY: Git down to brass tacks.
AMOS: Hello—Is you got any brass tacks?—I mean I got some brass tacks—No, wait a minute yere—(to Andy) Who's got some brass tacks, Andy?
ANDY: Not BRASS tacks—start de sy-rology on him.
AMOS: Hello—Mister—
ANDY: Start in on de sy-rology.
AMOS: Hello—How much do dat job pay?—You done had some kind o' notice in de paper—say you wants a man—whut I wants to know is—how much do de job pay?—It do?—Well, sy-rology.
ANDY: Whut IS you talkin' 'bout?
AMOS: Hello, Mister—sy-rology.—Dat mean whutever you is payin', dat ain't enough.
ANDY: No, no—
AMOS: No—no—Lissen yere, Mister, I wants to git de job—I say-a—I wants to git de job—Wait a minute, wait a minute—hold de phone a minute—
ANDY: Whut's de matter?
AMOS: De gen'man wants to know if I ever done anything befo'—where wuz de las' place I worked.

ANDY: Use some sy-rology; tell him you don' care whether you git de job or not.

AMOS: He sez he don' care either—den he hung up de telephone.

ANDY: Lissen yere—you is got to start usin' sy-rology on de man.
AMOS: Where is I goin' git any sy-rology to use on him?
ANDY: Whut do de man want to know?
AMOS: De man wants to know where is de las' place I worked.
ANDY: Tell him you is still workin' dere.
AMOS: Hello Mister—I is still workin' at de las' place I worked at—
ANDY: Talk up to de man.
AMOS: I kin do anything, Mister—
ANDY: Tell de man to hold de phone a minute.
AMOS: Hello Mister—will you hold de phone once mo' please—say—jest a minute.
ANDY: Now lissen yere, Amos—de trouble wid you is—you is beggin' de man fur de job—You is got use some sy-rology—den de sy-rology will start eatin' on de man's brain.
AMOS: De sy-rology'll start eatin' on de man's brain, huh?
ANDY: Now, go ahaid—use some sy-rology.
AMOS: Hello Mister—dis yere's Amos—dis yere's Amos Jones—
ANDY: Use some sy-rology—tell him you don' care whether you git de job or not.
AMOS: Hello Mister—I got sumpin' to tell you—Dis yere's Amos—You know dat job dat you done had in de paper?—well, I don' care whether I git it or not—Uh-huh. Hello—hello!—
ANDY: Whut's de matter?
AMOS: He say he don' care either—den he hung up de telephone.

ANDY: He done hung up, huh?
AMOS: I tol' him jest whut you tol' me to tell him —den he hung up de telephone.
ANDY: Dat's a'right—you done used sy-rology anyway. Now, you know whut's li'ble to happen?
AMOS: Whut's li'ble to happen now?
ANDY: Dat sy-rology dat you done used on him will start eatin' on his brain an' eat his brain up.
AMOS: Den he's li'ble to furgit about me wantin' dat job, ain't he?
ANDY: 'Tain't no use to 'splain nothin' to you Amos—
AMOS: I know—but I wants de job. I wants de job—

IX

Up to the present time Amos and Andy have been unable to secure work in Chicago. As we find the boys now they are on the verge of entering a butcher shop where a sign appears in the window—"Wanted a Window-washer."

Amos: Wait a minute yere now, Andy, befo' we go in dat place dere.
Andy: Now lissen yere, son—ain't no use to wait. Dere's a sign right dere in de window says—"Wanted, a Window-washer."
Amos: You wuz talkin' 'bout goin' to de inside o' de window. Dat's where all de ham is.
Andy: Dere you go now, you see. You don't 'preciates nothin'. I is trying to help you. I'se goin' let you wash de outside o' de window an' I'se goin' wash de inside.
Amos: Dat man ain't goin' let you eat none o' dat ham though when you gits in dere.
Andy: I ain't goin' eat none o' de ham. All I wants to do is to git a good smell of it, dat's all.
Amos: Let's go on in an' see de man.
Andy: Well, come on now—lemme do de talkin' in dere.
Amos: I hope dat man let us sample de ham while we'se in dere. Two-three slices o' ham would fix me up right, right now.

ANDY: Now when we git in dere—don't look like you is hungry.

AMOS: If I look natch'ral I'll look like I'se starvin' to death, I tell you dat.

ANDY: You is li'ble to git in de sto' dere an' start lookin' at one o' dem hams an' have a fit or sumpin'.

AMOS: If I don't git some ham or sumpin' in me pretty soon, I goin' drop over though.

ANDY: Now, git on in de sto' dere now an' let's talk to de man about gittin' dis job washin' de windows.

AMOS: Come on in wid me. You do de talkin'.

ANDY: Yere's de man right over yere.

AMOS: Go ahaid—ast de man.

MAN: Can I wait on you boys?

AMOS: Yas sah, Mister—Andy yere will tell you whut we want.

ANDY: Yas sah, Mister—I sees a sign in de window dat you want a window washer.

AMOS: Yas sah, dat's whut we come in yere fur.

MAN: Oh yes, you want to see the proprietor. Just a minute—I'll tell him you're here.

AMOS: Thank you sah, Mister, thank you sah. We'll wait right yere.

ANDY: I ain't never seed so much meat befo' at one time in my life.

AMOS: Look at de po'k chops yere in dis glass case.

ANDY: Sliced ham—po'k chops—look at dat sausage.

AMOS: If you stay in yere a while an' smell dis stuff, you might 'fresh yoreself up a little bit.

ANDY: Look at dat man back dere wid dat machine

back dere slicin' dat ham off. Look at dem slices peelin' off dere.

Amos: Dis yere's a good place to work a'right if de man don't care about you eatin' a piece o' ham now an' den.

Andy: I better take *dis* job 'cause I kin see now dat you ain't goin' be able to handle a big job like dis.

Amos: Whut you mean—you ain't goin' let me do half de work yere, huh?

Andy: Whut I is doin', Amos, is lookin' out fur you. I don' wants to see nothin' happen to you. You see I is stronger dan you is. You'se li'ble to come down yere an' work yoreself to death an' git sick or sumpin'.

Amos: How come you jest think o' dat?

Andy: Well, when we fust saw de sign I thought dat one window dere was de only one but look at all dese show cases yere.

Amos: Dat's whut I likes about it—all dese show cases.

Andy: 'Tain't no use fur you to git on no job like dis.

Amos: Dat man is done told de boss 'bout us but de boss is busy. Look at him back dere.

Andy: De boss look like he's countin' money. Maybe up yere in Chicago dey pays you in re-vance.

Amos: I wish somebody would pay us sumpin'.

Andy: De trouble is wid you—you gits un-patient too quick.

Amos: If I had sumpin' to eat I wouldn't git un-patient.

Andy: Yere you is standin' right in de middle of a lot o' ham—

Amos: But de ham ain't doin' ME no good dere. I got have some ham in de middle o' me—dat's whut I got do.

Andy: Now lissen yere—*I'll* take dis job washin' dese windows an' dese show cases where all de ham is an' den at night when I finish washin' up de stuff 'round yere I'll ast de boss to gimme de ham bones.

Amos: You can't do nothin' wid no hambone. You got have some meat on it.

Andy: We kin make soup out de hambone.

Amos: I know, but you got have a little piece o' meat in de soup.

Andy: Maybe de boss will gimme a little meat.

Amos: Dis yere smell is 'bout to drive me crazy. I got git me sumpin' to eat, dat's whut I got do.

Andy: You better save whut little money you IS got now.

Amos: You tol' me if I come up to Chicago, people was goin' grab us an' put us to work.

Andy: De trouble wid you is—you ain't give de peoples up yere time enough to know we'se in town.

Amos: I'd carry a sign 'round on my back if it do any good.

Andy: I wish dat man would come on up yere an' gimme de job.

Amos: Dis yere's de fust time I ever saw YOU want a job.

Andy: De thing I wants to do is to git YOU a job. But it ain't no use to git you a job 'round a lot o' meat. You can't eat a lot o' meat up yere in dis kind o' weather.

Amos: Whut's de weather got do wid me eatin' meat?
Andy: In de fust place, diff'ent parts o' de country, you eats diff'ent things. If you git yoreself a box o' crackers an' two-three glasses o' water, you'll fill right up.
Amos: Dat ain't doin' me no good though.
Andy: Now, when dis man come up yere, I goin' tell you again—don't look like you is hungry.
Amos: I b'lieve I'll git myself ten cents worth o' dis ham while I'se waitin' fur de man. Git yoreself ten cents worth too.
Andy: Ain't no use fur both of us to buy ten cents worth o' ham. You go ahaid, git ten cents worth. I jest wants a little nibble.
Amos: You jest wants a little nibble, huh? I goin' ast dis man yere.
Andy: Go ahaid, ast him.
Amos: Mister, while we'se waitin' yere will you sell me ten cents worth o' dat ham, please sah?
Man: You want ten cents worth of this sliced ham?
Amos: Yas sah, Yas sah—gimme ten cents worth o' dat sliced ham right now, please sah.
Andy: Dat ham look pretty good, don't it?
Amos: Why don't *you* buy ten cents worth?
Andy: I don't want no ham. I'll take a little nibble off o' yourn.
Amos: You don't git MUCH o' dat stuff fur ten cents, do you? Dat's a'right, Mister—don't wrap it up *too* tight—I goin' git right in it.
Man: There you are.
Amos: Yere's de ten cents, Mister.
Andy: You better gimme a slice o' dat—lemme see how it taste.

Amos: Yere you is—take a little piece.
Andy: Well, dem two slices stuck together—I'll jest take dem two.
Amos: How do it taste?
Andy: Dis yere's GOOD ham.
Amos: I b'lieve I'll eat a slice.
Andy: Wait a minute, wait a minute—don't eat de stuff in de man's sto'.
Amos: You is eatin' it in yere.
Andy: When I wuz eatin' it, de man wasn't lookin'.
Amos: Whut mus' I do wid it—put it in my pocket?
Andy: Better gimme one mo' slice 'fore you wrap it up.
Amos: I thought you wuz jest goin' nibble on it.
Andy: Put de ham in yore pocket—yere come de man.
Man: You boys waiting to see me?
Andy: Yas sah, Mister. I sees a sign in de window dere says you wants a window washer.
Amos: Yas sah, we done see de sign—dat's how we come in.
Andy: Shut up—I'se talkin' to de gen'man.
Man: Which one of you boys is a good window washer?
Andy: I is de window washer, Mister. Amos yere is jest wid me, dat's all. I is one o' de best window washers you done ever seed.
Amos: Yas sah, Mister, Andy yere's de best one, I guess, but I know a little sumpin' 'bout it too.
Andy: I'll take de job myself, Mister. I knows all about washin' windows.
Man: If you make a good job of this I'll let you come here and wash them twice a week. It will take you all day to wash them—that will be

two days a week—I'll pay you four dollars a day. Now, you wash the windows Tuesday and Friday. So you can start right in now if you want to.

ANDY: Dat suits me.

AMOS: You ain't got no mo' windows you wants washed nowhere, is you?

ANDY: Don't pay no 'tention to him, Mister. (To Amos) Why don't you shut up?

MAN: Now wait here a minute and I'll get you the rope.

ANDY: Yas sah—yas sah. (To Amos) Whut did he say he wuz goin' git?

AMOS: He either said soap or rope.

ANDY: I hope it IS *soap*.

AMOS: I ain't never heerd o' washin' no windows wid rope befo'. Maybe de man is talkin' 'bout a mop made out o' rope.

ANDY: Dat las' thing de man say sounds bad. Wait a minute—yere come de man.

MAN: Now, here you are.

ANDY: Yere I is, huh?

AMOS: Is dat whut you goin' wash de window wid, dat stuff?

MAN: You see, I own this five story building and I want to get these windows upstairs washed. Now all you do is to put this rope around your waist.

ANDY: I puts it 'round my waist, huh?

MAN: That's right—and you can start up on the fifth floor. Just be careful when you are washing the outside because these hooks clamp on some fasteners on the outside of the window but that wood up there is kind o' rotten. Just be

sure that you don't put too much strain on it.
ANDY: Wait a minute, Mister. I b'lieve Amos yere is a better window washer dan I is.
AMOS: Wait a minute yere—I ain't goin' wash no windows yere—I ain't goin' do dat, no sah, I ain't goin' do dat—

X

Amos and Andy find their funds getting very low and decide to start cooking at home. They borrow a little stove from the landlord's wife and, as we find the boys now, Amos is just returning from the grocery store with a few packages.

Amos: Yere I is, Andy—I got de stuff yere.
Andy: Well—It took you long enough to go down dere an' git dat stuff.
Amos: I knows it did, Andy, but I got down to de grocery store an' furgot whut you send me after.
Andy: Let's git busy yere an' git to cookin'.
Amos: Yere's de stuff right yere. I got a can o' beans—some cauliflower—a loaf o' bread.
Andy: You didn't git no meat, did you?
Amos: Meat cost too much—I ain't got enough money to git no meat wid.
Andy: Whut is dis?—cauliflower?
Amos: Yeah—I got ten cents worth o' cauliflower.
Andy: Is dat all de cauliflower de man give you fur ten cents?
Amos: Dat's all he gimme. I give him ten cents fur it.
Andy: We got cook dis cauliflower.
Amos: I know—dat's goin' take de longest of all to

cook. Dese yere beans, all we got do is heat 'em.

ANDY: I'se so hungry dat I ain't got time to wait fur dat cauliflower. You ought to got two cans o' beans—dat's whut you ought to done.

AMOS: All I got wuz a loaf o' bread, an' de beans, an' de cauliflower.

ANDY: You *knows* I likes meat.

AMOS: I likes meat too but de man ain't givin' it away. Meat cost money.

ANDY: De thing we got do yere is to heat dem beans up 'cause I is plen'y hungry.

AMOS: You ain't no hungrier dan I is.

ANDY: Well, don't argue so much—git de beans in de pan dere an' light dat stove.

AMOS: You ain't got no can opener, is you?

ANDY: Whut you think I do—carry a can opener 'round wid me?

AMOS: Wait a minute—Yere's one right yere—I be doggoned. De lan' lord's wife done brought one in.

ANDY: Ain't no use to try to cook dat cauliflower now—dat's goin' take too long.

AMOS: I kin save dat cauliflower an' cook dat tomorrow.

ANDY: You kin git up in de mornin' an' cook dat an' have it all ready fur me when I git up.

AMOS: You ain't plannin' on eatin' cauliflower fur breakfast, is you?

ANDY: I got have some ham an' eggs in de mornin' somewhere.

AMOS: Where we goin' git any ham an' eggs in de mornin'? First thing you know yere we goin' spend ev'vy dime we got.

ANDY: Well, go ahaid, cook de beans now. Don't git me mad now—don't git me mad.
AMOS: Lemme git dis can o' beans open yere now—we goin' eat some beans.
ANDY: If you'd git a job yere, we could make some money.
AMOS: How is I goin' git a job—I can't find none. You ought to take dat job washin' de windows, dat's whut you ought to taken.
ANDY: You heard whut dat man say, didn't you?
AMOS: I heard de man say he wanted you to wash de windows on de fifth floor.
ANDY: Dat man gimme dat rope to put 'round my waist yere an' told me to hook it on dem hooks up dere on de outside o' de window. Den he told me not to put too much strain on it 'cause de wood was rotten an' dem hooks was li'ble to pull out.
AMOS: I know one thing—I ain't goin' wash no windows dat high off de ground.
ANDY: Dem beans smells pretty good—I b'lieve I could eat 'em cold.
AMOS: Wait a minute yere now—lemme git 'em kind of warm—dey'se better when dey'se warm.
ANDY: I smells gas.
AMOS: I kind of smells gas too. De gas IS 'scapin' somewhere, ain't it?
ANDY: Maybe dat hose runnin' to de stove is leakin'.
AMOS: Dat's jist whut 'tis—look yere, put yore nose up yere.
ANDY: I ain't goin' put my nose up to dat hose an' smell no gas.
AMOS: Go ahaid—smell it.

ANDY: I ain't goin' let no gas go up my nose. I ain't goin' git 'fixinated.
AMOS: Whut you mean—'fixinated?
ANDY: If dat gas git up yore nose, you goin' git 'fixinated.
AMOS: 'Splain dat big word to me—whut do it mean?
ANDY: You go ahead, smell dat gas a little while. Den when you gits 'fixinated, I'll 'splain it to you.
AMOS: I don't guess dat gas is 'scapin' enough to blow up nothin' 'round here is it?
ANDY: Go ahaid, light de stove.
AMOS: Well, yere goes—git out de way now—'case dis yere thing blows I goin' blow jest 'fore it do.
ANDY: Dere you is—dere you is—ain't nothin' wrong wid dat now—see dere. Yere we is, yere nearly starved to death—got a can o' beans an' a loaf o' bread. Didn't you git no butter?
AMOS: You ain't gimme no money to git no butter wid.
ANDY: I thought you'd have enough sense to git butter.
AMOS: I ain't got no money to be buyin' no butter wid.
ANDY: Wait a minute yere—hand me a pencil an' a piece o' paper. I is got to figger.
AMOS: Go ahaid, figger—whut you goin' figger?
ANDY: How much money is you got left?
AMOS: I got a doller an' sixty cents. How much is you got?
ANDY: Dat ain't none o' yore bizness.
AMOS: Well, I done told you how much *I* got
ANDY: Dat's 'cause I'se figgerin'.

AMOS: You got 'bout fo'—five dollers though. You ain't done spent as much money as I is.
ANDY: You gotta doller an' sixty cents. Well, 'cordin' to my figures yere, dat ain't goin' last us.
AMOS: Dat ain't goin' last us where?
ANDY: Dat ain't goin' keep us in food but a couple o' days.
AMOS: Wait a minute yere though—you talkin' 'bout us. Ain't you countin' on spendin' yore money?
ANDY: We got hold down on food yere, boy. I is plen'y hungry, I know dat.
(Knock on door.)
ANDY: Come in—come in.
AMOS: Hello dere, Mr. Washington.
WASH: Hello dere, boys. My wife told me to bring you in dis letter. I b'lieve it's fur you, Amos.
AMOS: Thank you, Mr. Washington, thank you.
WASH: My wife wants to know if you boys is cumftubble—if you got plen'y covers an' everything.
ANDY: Yas sah, tell her we is alright.
AMOS: Yas sah, we gittin' 'long a'right, Mr. Washington.
WASH: We jest finished eatin' a great big roast beef. We was goin' ast you boys over but we didn't think of it.
AMOS: Dat's a'right, sah, dat's a'right.
ANDY: You didn't think of it—dat's too bad.
WASH: We had a good roast today—nice an' juicy. Well, boys—I'll see you later.
AMOS: A'right, Mr. Washington—goo'bye.
ANDY: Juicy roast beef—Um—um.
AMOS: I got a letter yere from George down in At-

lanta. Dey done forwarded it over yere from General Delivery.

ANDY: Read me whut he say. Hurry up, 'cause I'se gittin' hungry.

AMOS: He say-a—wait a minute yere—Hello, Amos—how is you?—I saw yore sweetheart Mamie las' night on her way to a bar—ba—cue.

ANDY: Barbacue.

AMOS: I hope she wuz goin' wid a girl.

ANDY: Don't start talkin' 'bout Mamie now—read de rest o' de letter.

AMOS: Den he say yere—I wuz goin' go de bar-ba-cue but I had done ate so much roast po'k fur supper dat I was full so I didn't go.

ANDY: He's full o' roast po'k, huh?

AMOS: Dat certainly do make you hungry, don't it?

ANDY: Juicy roast beef—barbacue an' roast po'k. Read on.

AMOS: Write me an' let me know how things is wid you boys—I am goin' over to Maggie's house tonight wid some of de boys. Dey is havin' a big chicken dinner.

ANDY: Dat's enough—don't read no mo'.

AMOS: Dat gas is smellin' funny—I b'lieve we'se gittin' 'fixinated.

ANDY: Dat gas DO smell funny now. What's de matter?

AMOS: Look yere Andy—de beans done burned up.

ANDY: *Whut is de matter wid you?*

AMOS: I couldn't help de beans burnin' up—don't hit me, don't hit me—

XI

Amos and Andy, being hard pressed for funds, are trying very hard to secure work. Andy arranged for Amos to get a job as an iron worker but when Amos found out an iron worker's duty he quickly decided not to be one. As the scene opens now we find the boys en route home just after leaving the place where a skyscraper is under construction. It was there that Amos saw an iron worker riding a beam being hoisted on top of the building by a large derrick.

AMOS: Ain't no use to talk to me—I ain't goin' be no iron worker.
ANDY: Dat job dat I wuz goin' git you as a iron worker pays big money.
AMOS: I don't care if dey gimme a hundred dollars a week. If I'd ever fall off one o' dem things, de money ain't goin' do me no good.
ANDY: De trouble wid you is—you is scared to work.
AMOS: I'se scared to work dat high off de GROUND. Why don't YOU git a job as a iron worker?
ANDY: I ain't built fur a iron worker. I'se big—I'se too big.
AMOS: You can't fall no harder dan I kin.
ANDY: Well, I done come to one 'clusion.
AMOS: Dat don't make no diff'ence, Andy—I'll come

to one too but I ain't goin' be no iron worker.

ANDY: I done 'cided dat you would ruther starve to death dan to go to work.

AMOS: No I wouldn't. I willin' to do anythin'. I'll sweep de streets, do anythin' to do a honest livin'—but don't git me way up in de air where I can't keep my feet on de ground—dat's de main thing I got do.

ANDY: A iron worker gits good money an' de comp'ny looks out fur him.

AMOS: Whut you mean, de comp'ny looks out fur him? 'Splain dat to me.

ANDY: De comp'ny dat 'ploys you insures yore life de minute you start work. Now lissen, 'spose you'd fall off de buildin'—you is re-sured. Yore benifisher git $10,000.

AMOS: I ain't leavin' no money to no fishes. Whut good is $10,000 goin' do me when I'se laying down on de sidewalk wid my haid bust open?

ANDY: Re-surance is de bes' thing in de world.

AMOS: I ain't arguin' wid you 'bout it—but it ain't doin' ME no good. I don't care nothin' 'bout de baby-fishes either.

ANDY: Well, de way you is goin' yere, you ain't *never* goin' git a job.

AMOS: We GOT git a job somewhere.

ANDY: Can't you write some o' yore friends down in Atlanta an' borrow some money?

AMOS: I can't borrow money from none of 'em.

ANDY: We got borrow some money from somewhere befo' dis yere week is over.

AMOS: De only one dat I know down dere dat thinks anything o' me is Mamie. I ain't goin' ast her fur no money. I ain't writ her but two post cards since I been yere.

ANDY: Why don't you write Mamie's mama a letter?—an' tell her mama dat you is swingin' a big deal up yere.

AMOS: I can't write Mamie's mama an' ast her fur no money. Dey takes all de money dey kin work fur to keep livin'.

ANDY: Well, we got git a hold o' some money or a job or sumpin'.

AMOS: You tol' me if I come up yere dat de jobs was layin' 'round yere. Yere we is up yere now—can't even find one.

ANDY: Now, don't be un-patient—don't be un-patient.

AMOS: I ain't gittin' un-patient—I jist wants to git a job, dat's all.

ANDY: Wait a minute yere now—let's stop walkin' yere an' sit down a minute yere. Lemme git my pencil out.

AMOS: Whut is you goin' do—start figgerin' some mo'?

ANDY: If it wasn't fur me figgerin' yere you'd NEVER git a job. I'se tryin' to he'p you yere now—I'se goin' figger.

AMOS: Whut you goin' figger now?

ANDY: Lemme see yere now. How much money is you got?

AMOS: I got a doller an' ten cents.

ANDY: Lemme put dat down yere—one doller an' ten cents—Amos is got.

AMOS: Whut is you figgerin' now—'splain it to me—whut is you figgerin'?

ANDY: Don't holler at me like dat—can't you see

me standin' yere tryin' to consolate on dese figgers?

AMOS: 'Scuse me—I didn't mean to holler at you.

ANDY: Amos is got—one doller an' ten cents.

AMOS: Dat's ALL Amos is got too.

ANDY: You goin' keep on hollerin' till I hit you in de nose. Shut up now an' lemme figger.

AMOS: Go ahead—figger.

ANDY: 'Cordin' to dese figgers yere dat I got—wait a minute now—lemme re-check.

AMOS: Go ahaid—re-check—I wants to know whut you done figgered.

ANDY: If egg-san'wiches cost ten cents a-piece, an' you kin live on one egg san'wich a day, you kin keep goin' fur 'leven days.

AMOS: Is dat how it come out?

ANDY: Dat's 'cordin' to my figgers yere—an' when I figgers, I figgers—I don't mess wid 'em.—So you ain't so bad off.

AMOS: You know we ain't paid de room rent fur las' week yit.

ANDY: Dat's right—you *ain't* paid de room-rent, is you?

AMOS: Whut you mean, *I* ain't paid it? YOU is 'sposed to pay it too, ain't you?

ANDY: Well, I tell you whut we kin do—

AMOS: Whut KIN we do?

ANDY: You ast de lan'lord if we can't stan' him off a week. Tell him you is 'spectin' to git a lot o' money.

AMOS: I can't tell de man no story 'bout it—I AIN'T 'spectin' to git a lot o' money. De way things is goin' yere, I'se 'spectin' to starve to death—dat's whut I'se 'spectin' to do.

ANDY: Ain't neither one of us got no—no-a—— no-a———liquid assets.
AMOS: I don't want nothin' to drink—I got git a job, dat's whut I got do.
ANDY: Amos—I kin see 'tain't no use to try to talk bizness to you. De older you gits, de dumber you gits.
AMOS: You know we got pay de room rent.
ANDY: We kin work dat out wid de lan'lord. Let him hold yore suitcase.
AMOS: Oh, I don't think we goin' have no trouble wid him. I was talkin' to de lan'lady an' her husband yistidday—an' dey knows we is kind of up again it.
ANDY: Well, den, if dey KNOW we'se up again it—don't let's pay 'em. Let 'em wait.
AMOS: We can't take 'vantage of 'em like dat jest 'cause dey wants to see us git along—it ain't no use to take 'vantage of 'em.
ANDY: De trouble wid you is—you is chicken hearted. If we kin stall de lan'lady fur two-three weeks, let's do it.
AMOS: If I can't pay de lan'lady whut I owe her inside o' two weeks, I goin' give her ever'thing I got an' start walkin' back to Atlanta, dat's whut I goin' do.
ANDY: Now wait a minute yere, Amos—I'se yore buddy—you ain't plannin' on leavin' yore buddy flat, is you?
AMOS: You ain't no flatter dan *I* is, Andy—dis yere thing is gittin' serious now.
ANDY: Whut we got do is stick together.
AMOS: I know we got stick together. We got git some work though.

ANDY: De thing I got do is to git myself a office job.
AMOS: Whut you mean—you'll git yoreself a office job—you mean cleanin' up de office or sumpin'?
ANDY: No-no—see, a man dat is smart as I is ain't got no bizness doin' no heavy work. I ought to be de head executor in a big comp'ny.
AMOS: I don't guess I'll ever have enough sense to do nothin' like dat—whutever dat is.
ANDY: I would start a comp'ny of my own an' give you a job but de trouble is, I need a little money to start on.
AMOS: Whut kind o' bizness would you start out wid?
ANDY: Well, I'd open up some kind o' factory an' make sumpin'.
AMOS: De fust thing we better make is some ham san'wiches—dat's whut we better do.
ANDY: Come on—let's walk down yere in front o' de barber shop—we know two—three o' de boys down dere.
AMOS: I wish we could git a job. By de way, I met one o' de boys dat lives 'cross de street from us—his name is Sylvester. He tol' me dat jobs was kind of hard to git right now.
ANDY: Where did you meet de boy?
AMOS: As I wuz comin' out de grocery store, we bumped into each other an' I stepped on his foot or sumpin'. I thought he wuz goin' git mad but he was nice about it—so he walked back up to de house wid me. I tol' him I wuz from Atlanta and he say dat jobs is hard to git.
ANDY: Dere you go now—talkin' to ever'body you see—don't tell ever'body yore bizness. Dis yere

boy Sylvester is li'ble to be a pickpocket fur all you know. He's li'ble to be a bad man.

Amos: If I would run into de meanest man in de world, I couldn't lose but a doller an' ten cents. Sylvester tol' me dat if we wuz broke an' couldn't pay de room rent, his mama would give us a room till we could git on our feet.

Andy: Maybe Sylvester ain't so bad. Don't furgit where he live.

Amos: Yere's de barber shop. You wants to go on in dere?

Andy: Well, I don' know whut we goin' do after we git in dere. Let's sit down yere on dis box.

Amos: Dis yere boy Sylvester dat I was tellin' you 'bout—he seemed to be a nice boy—'bout nineteen years old, I guess.

Andy: Maybe if his ole lady'll give us a room fur nothin', she might give us sumpin' to eat fur nothin'. We could go over to his house an' stay over dere.

Amos: We can't do dat. I ain't got de heart to 'pose on 'em like dat.

Andy: You gits me so mad some times I don' know whut to do wid you. Yere we is now—got a chance to eat an' sleep fur nothin' an' you don' wants to do it.

Amos: I jest met de boy—I don' know him—I don' know his mama or nothin'. Dat wouldn't be right fur us to go down dere widout payin' sumpin'.

Andy: Amos, you ain't treatin' me right. Jest 'cause one o' yore friends offers to let us sleep an' eat down dere, you claim you don' wants to do it.

Amos: To tell you de truth, Andy, I wouldn't feel

right stayin' down dere widout payin' fur it. Even if his mama 'sisted on it, I wouldn't stay down dere less I paid her fur it.

ANDY: Dat's crazy—now listen yere—dat's why you ain't got nothin' now. Lemme tell you sumpin'. Whenever you git a chance to git anything fur nothin'—take it.

AMOS: I'd ruther starve to death dan do sumpin' like dat—I ain't got de heart to do it, dat's all.

ANDY: You gits me re-gusted.

AMOS: Look who's comin' yere—I be doggoned.

ANDY: Who is it?

AMOS: Yere come Sylvester right down de street now. Dat's de boy I been tellin' you 'bout. He's jest a young boy.

ANDY: In-reduce me to him.

AMOS: Hello, Sylvester—how is you?

SYL: Hello, Mr. Amos—how is you?

AMOS: I'se pretty good, Sylvester—I wants you to meet my buddy yere—dis yere's Andy, Sylvester.

ANDY: Glad I met you.

SYL: I glad to know you, Mr. Andy. Well, Mr. Amos—whut is you doin' down yere—I'se jest goin' in to git a hair cut.

AMOS: I was jest tellin' Andy 'bout you, Sylvester.

ANDY: I got a little matter I wants to talk over wid you.

SYL: Yas sah—yas sah.

AMOS: You go ahaid—git yore hair cut—we'll see you when yore finish.

ANDY: I'll 'range fur us to move over to his house—room an' board fur nothin'—dat's whut we got git. . . .

XII

Amos and Andy went down town to see about a job. After being told that the work was very easy and consisted of only sitting in a chair a few hours as a watchman Andy decided to take the job himself until he discovered that he was in an undertaking establishment assigned as night watchman of the morgue. Both boys immediately left. As we find them now they are on their way back home.

AMOS: I thought dat one of us wuz goin' git a job at dat las' place. I didn't even know where we wuz, did you?
ANDY: No sah, son—but when I looked through dat door an' saw de morgue, dat wuz enough fur me.
AMOS: I don't blame you 'bout dat. I ain't goin' mess 'round no undertaker's place neither.
ANDY: I ruther git a job paintin' flag poles dan I would bein' a night watchman in a undertaker's place.
AMOS: In de fust place, a undertaker's place is full o' hants.
ANDY: It's mo' hants in a undertaker's place dan any place in de world.
AMOS: I'se scared o' hants too—I ain't goin' mess 'round none of 'em. I'se still scared—I don't guess I goin' be able to go to sleep tonight.

ANDY: If you wants to take dat job, you kin go back down dere an' take it but not me.

AMOS: I don't want de job—I ain't goin' fool 'round no morgue.

ANDY: De man say all you got do is sit dere.

AMOS: Till one o' dem hants come out o' dere an' grab me—I know—I ain't goin' mess wid it.

ANDY: A hant can't HURT you.

AMOS: I ain't goin' let none of 'em git dat close to me.

ANDY: Some o' dem dead people's in dere's jest been dead a few days.

AMOS: Dat's jest a few days too long to me.

ANDY: De man said he would lock de front do' so nobody could git in.

AMOS: If he gits me down dere he better let dat front do' open so I kin git out o' dere.

ANDY: Ain't no use to git scared about de place.

AMOS: I ain't gittin' scared 'bout it. I'se jest makin' certain, dat's all.

ANDY: Whut you mean, you makin' certain?

AMOS: I'm makin' certain dat I ain't goin' back dere, dat's all.

ANDY: I is havin' a hard time gittin' a job fur you, you know dat, don't you?

AMOS: De trouble is—all de jobs is dangerous. One job dat you was talkin' 'bout—dat iron worker—ridin' dem big iron pieces up on de twen'y-sev'nth floor—messin' 'round a undertaker.

ANDY: Now lissen yere, son—de thing we got do is start figgerin'. How much money is you got left?

AMOS: I got 65 cents now.

The boys left there immediately.

ANDY: De thing you better do is take out some re-surance.
AMOS: Re-surance against whut?
ANDY: Starvin' to death.
AMOS: I got git myself a job—dat's whut I got do.
ANDY: De thing we got do is to move over to Sylvester's house. If he said dat his mama will feed us an' give us a room, dat's de thing to do.
AMOS: I ain't goin' move over to Sylvester's house as long as I'se able to work.
ANDY: Well, you ain't got but 65 cents.
AMOS: I know I ain't got but 65 cents.
ANDY: You got make dat do now.
AMOS: I can't make it do no mo' dan it *do* do.
ANDY: Maybe we ought to go down to de 'ployment agency.
AMOS: I'll go down dere wid you but dey ain't got no job—I kin tell you dat. Ever'time dat dat man put up on de board dat dey need one man, 'bout seven hund'ed men start a fight to see who'll git it.
ANDY: Lemme see yere now—maybe I could write a letter to de secketary o' de Labor Interior.
AMOS: Whut good's dat goin' do us?
ANDY: Tell de Labor Interior man de sitiation yere.
AMOS: Well, go ahaid—write de letter if dat'll do any good.
ANDY: You ain't got no pen an' ink wid you, has you?
AMOS: No, I ain't got no pen an' ink wid me. I got a pencil yere if you wants to use dat.
ANDY: Is you got a piece o' paper?
AMOS: I got a piece o' wrappin' paper yere. Yere 'tis but it's dirty.

ANDY: I b'lieve I WILL write de secketary o' de Interior o' Labor.
AMOS: Whut you goin' tell him?
ANDY: Let's stop yere an' sit down yere a minute.
AMOS: Yere's de piece o' paper—go ahaid—write.
ANDY: Yere—you sit down dere now—write on yore knee—I'll de-tate de letter.
AMOS: Whut you mean?—whut you goin' do?
ANDY: As I call it out, you put it down.
AMOS: Go ahaid—I'se ready—I say—go ahaid, I'se ready.
ANDY: Don't holler at me like dat when I'se gittin' ready to de-tate.
AMOS: Whut mus' I say to de man?
ANDY: Start out—say—dear—secketary o' de Interior o' Labor.
AMOS: I ain't got enough paper to put all dat down.
ANDY: Don't git me mad now—write down whut I done tol' you.
AMOS: Whut is all dat again?
ANDY: Dear secketary of de Interior o' Labor—
AMOS: How you spell "dear secketary o' de Interior o' Labor"?
ANDY: D-double e—r—dear-a—s—s—s
AMOS: How many s's in dat thing?
ANDY: In whut thing?
AMOS: In dat word you is essin'.
ANDY: I ain't got but one s down dere—I ain't said but one "s".
AMOS: You said s—s—s.
ANDY: Dat shows you how dumb you is. Dat was de same "s" I was essin' over again.
AMOS: Start at de beginnin' again—take it again.

ANDY: Dear secketary o' de Interior o' Labor.
AMOS: I done heerd you say dat.
ANDY: Well, put it down. It's got e's an' c's an' t's an' y's in it.
AMOS: De main thing is though, how you gonna routine 'em.
ANDY: Start over.
AMOS: Don't make no diff'ence if I start over or if I go from where I is—I got de same thing.
ANDY: You ain't got nothin' yet. Start de letter over.
AMOS: Mus' I scratch out whut I got down yere?
ANDY: Scratch out ever'thing you got down dere.
AMOS: I'll scratch out dis dear seck den. Now, go ahaid, start over.
ANDY: You ready to start now?
AMOS: I'se ready—go ahaid.
ANDY: Say-a—dear seck.
AMOS: I jest scratched dat out.
ANDY: Well, scratch it in again.
AMOS: D—double e—r dear—s-e-c—seck—dear seck.
ANDY: Dear seck—
AMOS: Dear seck.
ANDY: You got dat down, ain't you?
AMOS: You mean 'bout callin' him a dear seck?
ANDY: You ain't callin' de man nothin'—you is 'dressin' him.
AMOS: I is.
ANDY: Dear seck.
AMOS: Dear seck.
ANDY: Ain't no use to write dat man—git him all worried 'bout ever'thing.

AMOS: Maybe dat's a good idea—he'll git all worried an' ever'thing.
ANDY: Let's git on home den.
AMOS: Maybe dat IS best—dat we don't write him. Come on—I'se ready. Les go.

XIII

Sylvester introduced Amos and Andy to a young girl by the name of Ruby Taylor. Ruby took the boys for an automobile ride and during this ride Amos and Ruby had quite a lengthy conversation. As per his promise, Amos called up Ruby and during the conversation something was said which put Amos under the impression that Ruby's father would be glad to give him a job. As we find Amos and Andy now they are just leaving the store where Amos dropped in to use the telephone.

Amos: Dis yere Ruby Taylor's a sweet gal a'right, Andy—ain't no two ways 'bout dat.
Andy: If her ole man is goin' give you a job, she ain't bad. But if you is jest goin' sit 'round an' talk love talk to de gal all de time, den you better let her alone.
Amos: You see, her papa's got a lot o' money.
Andy: Whut do her old man do?
Amos: He do's a lot o' things. He's a contractor—he builds buildin's—den he got a store dat he sells clothes in—den I b'lieve he's got a garage or sumpin'.
Andy: Well, out o' dem three places, you ought be able to git a job. An' if Ruby is pullin' fur you, she kin make her ole man give you big money.

Amos: De only thing about it—I hate to go to her father an' git a job jest 'cause I know Ruby.

Andy: Dere you go again now.

Amos: Whut you mean, dere I go?

Andy: Whut dif'ence do it make to you how you git de job jest so you git one?

Amos: Now wait a minute now, Andy—quiet down now—don' git mad. Well, de thing I'd like to do is git a job widout Ruby helpin' me if I could. I kind of feel funny goin' to her father jest 'cause she sent me up dere.

Andy: De thing you is got do now—you is got be smart.

Amos: Whut you mean, be smart?

Andy: You is got tell dis gal Ruby whut a big man *I* is an' git ME a job runnin' her papa's bizness fur him.

Amos: I can't git you no job runnin' her papa's bizness—he runs his own bizness I guess.

Andy: He needs a exe*cu*tive though like I is.

Amos: I don' know whut he needs.

Andy: If you work dis thing right wid dat gal, it won't take me long till I'm runnin' de ole man's bizness fur him.

Amos: Whut you mean, you goin' be runnin' his bizness?

Andy: I'll step in an' show de ole man dat I'se got a lot o' sense. Den he'll make me a big executor—den after I'm way up on top, I'll see dat *yore* work ain't so heavy.

Amos: De only trouble—I don't wants to go through Ruby jest to git myself in wid her papa—dat's de only trouble.

Andy: Now I tell you how we wants to work dis thing.
Amos: Go ahaid—how we goin' work it?
Andy: If dis yere Ruby Taylor don't say sumpin' to you in de nex' two—three days 'bout comin' over to her house to eat, den you better say to her-say-a—Miss Taylor, it would be very 'lightful to re-take o' some home-cooked groceries over at yore house.
Amos: Whut you mean—'vite myself over to her house?
Andy: Don't git excited now—don't git excited.
Amos: I ain't gittin' excited but I can't 'vite myself over to her house.
Andy: You kin make de re-gestion.
Amos: Whut's de use o' me gittin' sick?
Andy: Whut is you talkin' 'bout—gittin' sick?
Amos: You say sumpin' 'bout I could make myself have indigestion.
Andy: No, no,—you kin RE-GEST it to de gal.
Amos: Use some littler words. Whut is you talkin' 'bout?
Andy: Now lissen—now lissen now—you goes over to her house to eat—
Amos: How I goin' git over dere?
Andy: De nex' time you see her, start talkin' 'bout food.
Amos: She's li'ble to git hungry an' I ain't got but 'bout twenty cents.
Andy: No, no—tell her dat you like home cooked food.
Amos: You'se fixin' to git dat gal mad wid me.
Andy: Den when you git over to her house, you kin meet her papa.

Amos: I'll be scared to death if I meet her papa.

Andy: If her papa is a big man like I is, he smokes seegars so de thing to do is to give him a good seegar—de kind dat he smokes.

Amos: Where I goin' git any seegar from to give him?

Andy: De thing to do is to git over to his house befo' he gits dere an' when Ruby says to you—will you have one o' papa's seegars, take one or two of 'em—stick 'em in yore pocket—den when de ole man come home, give him one.

Amos: Give him one of his own seegars, huh?

Andy: Den you know you ain't makin' him mad by givin' him no bad tobacco. Dat's whut you call sy-rology again.

Amos: Dat's sy-rology, huh? De las' job I lost wuz on 'count o' dat sy-rology mess.

Andy: Now lissen—when her papa gits home, you is sittin' dere. You is all dressed up.

Amos: In whut?

Andy: In yore clothes.

Amos: I ain't got no mo' clothes 'cept de ones I got on. I can't dress up no mo' dan I is.

Andy: If you'll lissen to me, Amos, I'll tell you jest how to work it so dat you will be sittin' on top o' de sitiation while I is runnin' de ole man's bizness.

Amos: Wait a minute yere now—In de fust place Andy, I don' know Miss Taylor well enough to go over to her house.

Andy: She is crazy 'bout you. Couldn't you tell by dat look in her eye dat she likes you?

Amos: I was so 'cited when I wuz sittin' wid her

[84]

in de automobile dat I couldn't look her in de eye.

Andy: All you got do is to git in de house befo' her ole man gits home.

Amos: An' git arrested fur bein' a burglar or sumpin'—I ain't goin' do dat.

Andy: Jest keep yore haid now an' lissen to me.

Amos: Go ahaid den—I'se lissenin'.

Andy: Den when you is sittin' down at de table eatin', you casual'ty say—

Amos: I do whut say?

Andy: You CASUAL'TY.

Amos: I casual'ty, huh?

Andy: You casual'ty say to de old man—"how is bizness?" If you kin call him papa, you is better off dan you is callin' him sumpin' else.

Amos: He ain't no kin to me—I can't call him papa.

Andy: Yore ig'nance is even gittin' worse.

Amos: Go ahaid—I'm doin' de best I kin—'splain it to me.

Andy: Now, pitcher yoreself sittin' at de dinner table.

Amos: Dat's a pretty pitcher a'right—I'd like to be dere.

Andy: Whut is de fust thing you would say?

Amos: Please pass de food.

Andy: No-no—whut is you goin' do when you git dere?

Amos: Fill up on meat an' potatoes—or whutever dey has.

Andy: You is got git her papa on yore side.

Amos: Of de table?

Andy: Amos, sometimes I is goin' ketch you by de

nap o' de neck an' beat yore haid up against de wall.

AMOS: Don't git mad wid me now, Andy.

ANDY: De thing you is got do is to let her papa know dat you want a job, payin' big money—an' if he ain't got one, let him find one.

AMOS: You mean ast him to go down to de 'ployment agency fur me?

ANDY: No, lissen yere, Amos, lissen. Stop walkin'. You can't do two things at one time. You can't work yore haid an' yore feet. Stand still now. Dis Ruby Taylor has got a papa, ain't she?

AMOS: Yeah—she got a papa a'right.

ANDY: Her papa has got money, ain't he?

AMOS: Yeah—her papa got plen'y money, dey say.

ANDY: Her papa is a big bizness man.

AMOS: Yeah—her papa's a big bizness man.

ANDY: Now, you ain't got no money—you ain't got no job an' you ain't got no sense. Now, whut do you wants to do?

AMOS: Keep away from her papa.

ANDY: Keep on now, Amos—Keep on. I'se goin' give you a backhand lick in de mouth in a minute so hard dat you won't be able to shave fur two weeks.

AMOS: Please don't git mad wid me now, Andy—I'se tryin' to understan' whut you is talkin' 'bout—you is gittin' me mixed up.

ANDY: De thing you got do is to talk to her papa.

AMOS: About whut?

ANDY: About bizness.

AMOS: I don't know nuthin' 'bout her papa's bizness.

ANDY: Amos, you is SO dumb, you ought to sit down

in de street an' hit yoreself in de haid wid some rocks.

AMOS: Dat reminds me—I kin git myself a job dis summer, a fella tole me, out at Riverview, stickin' my head in a hole through a piece o' canvas an' let 'em throw baseballs at me.

ANDY: Shut up!

AMOS: Wait a minute now—don' git mad wid me— ain't no use to git mad.

XIV

Ruby Taylor left Amos and Andy a fried chicken which she sent over to their room by Sylvester. When the boys arrived in their room they found a note from Sylvester stating that he had put the chicken in the clothes basket and then the landlady informed the boys that the washwoman had just left with their clothes, consequently they lost the chicken. Both Amos' and Andy's mouths are watering for the fried chicken. As we find them now they are in their room —Andy is disgusted and Amos is discouraged.

AMOS: If Sylvester hadn't put dat chicken in dat clothes basket, we'd be eatin' chicken right now.
ANDY: Dat was de crazies' thing I ever heerd of.
AMOS: Ruby Taylor sent US de chicken an' den he put it in de clothes basket an' 'fore we kin git yere, de washwoman comes yere an' takes de dirty clothes out—chicken an' all. I guess Sylvester thought dat was a good place to put it.
ANDY: He ought to have better sense dan to put it in de clothes basket. Sometimes I t'inks dey ain't nobody in de world got any sense but me.
AMOS: I certainly would like to have some fried chicken right now. Um—um—whut I could do a leg an' de breast an' de neck an' de feet an' ever'thing else.

ANDY: Next time I see Sylvester I ought to smack him down.
AMOS: Don't git mad wid Sylvester now, Andy.—He thought he wuz doin' de right thing. He brought de chicken over yere—he was tryin' to hide it.
ANDY: He hided it a'right.
AMOS: Maybe we could go out to de washwoman's house an' git de chicken.
ANDY: I wish we COULD git it away from her.
AMOS: You know where de washwoman lives?
ANDY: Yeah—she jest lives two—three blocks from yere.
AMOS: Well, whut would we tell her when we git down dere?
ANDY: De thing to do is to tell her dat—lemme see now—we ought to have sumpin' legal 'bout dis so we'll scare her. Maybe she don't wants to give us dat chicken back.
AMOS: Dat IS right—maybe she won't give us de chicken back. Fried chickens is hard to git, you know.
ANDY: I wuz readin' some law de other day in a book somewheres. Lemme see now if I can't remember sumpin' to tell her.
AMOS: Think hard now.
ANDY: Lemme see—'cordin' to law, de books says dat re-possession is 'leven points o' de law.
AMOS: Re-possession is dat many points, huh?
ANDY: De chicken is in her re-possession now.
AMOS: She got de chicken a'right when she got de clothes—I know dat.
ANDY: Whut I got do is git legal—dat's whut I got do is git legal.

Amos: Whut you mean, you goin' git legal?
Andy: If we go over to her house after de chicken dat's goin' start argument. De thing I got do is to act like a lawyer.
Amos: You kin act like a lawyer if you wants to, can't you?
Andy: How long is she had de chicken?
Amos: Lemme think yere now—I guess she had it 'bout two hours. I guess she's savin' it fur dinner tomorrow. Dey'll have dat chicken fur Sunday dinner if we don't git over dere.
Andy: We got git over dere an' git dat chicken, dat's whut *we* got do. Gimme a pencil.
Amos: Yere you is—whut is you goin' do?—some figgerin'?
Andy: I got git de facts yere on dis thing in order to prove to de washwoman dat de chicken belong to us.
Amos: A'right—git de facts together dere now. We'll go over dere an' GIT dat chicken.
Andy: Whut is today?
Amos: Today is Sat'day—we got take a bath too, by de way.
Andy: Shut up! Today is Sat'day, ain't it?
Amos: Today is Sat'day—yeah, dat's right.
Andy: Dat's de fust thing I'll say to her. I'll walk up to her an' I'll say—'cordin' to law, today is Sat'day—an' if she's got dat chicken in her hands, she'll drop it right then.
Amos: You know law a'right. Ain't no two ways 'bout dat—I kin see de way you goin' after it.
Andy: Whut proof is de washwoman got dat we is done give her de chicken?
Amos: She ain't got NO proof.

ANDY: Dere you is right dere.
AMOS: Dat's de stuff—dat's de stuff—git all dat together.
ANDY: Be quiet now—lemme think sumpin'—lemme see yere.
AMOS: Whut is you tryin' to think of?
ANDY: I'se jest figgerin' yere if dere's anything in de consplution of de United States about fried chicken. Dey is in season a'right, ain't dey?
AMOS: Fried chicken is always in season.
ANDY: I got de day o' de week down yere a'right—Sat'day—I'se almost got enough stuff down yere right now to show her dat I is a lawyer.
AMOS: You goin' over dere an' tell her dat you is a lawyer, huh?
ANDY: I goin' let you do de talkin' to her an' I'll tell you 'zackly whut to say—den you talk to her an' tell her dat I is de lawyer.
AMOS: You goin' over dere wid me though, ain't you?
ANDY: I'll walk over dere wid you an' de fust thing you wants to say to her is-a—whut's de washwoman's name?
AMOS: De washwoman's name is Miz Lee.
ANDY: Miz Lee, huh?
AMOS: Dat's right—dat's right.
ANDY: Den de thing you wants to say—you wants to say-a—Miz Lee, on Sat'day of dis week, which, 'cordin' to law, is today, you has in yore re-possession, one fried chicken which flew dis way by mistake. 'Cordin' to law de chicken belongs to us 'cause by un-legal means of 'cedure de chicken got messed up in de clothes.

Amos: I ain't goin' never remember all dem big words.

Andy: Now lissen—fur once, git sumpin' in yore haid. Den after you says all dat, you looks over at me an' den you says to de washwoman—Miz Lee, Andrew Brown yere is a world re-knowed lawyer. Den I'll cough like dis—I'll say Ahem—Ahem.

Amos: I'se 'fraid I ain't goin' 'member all dat stuff—dat's de trouble.

Andy: De main thing we wants to do is to 'press her, wid de 'po'tance of me.

Amos: Why don't YOU talk to her?

Andy: De thing is I don' wants to talk to her—I wants to let her think dat I is too big to be talkin' to her.

Amos: You could git de thing right—I might git it mixed up.

Andy: All you got do is to remember two things—an' den we'll come back yere an' eat fried chicken. I wants her to think dat I is a big man—see. I is now gonna ast you questions like de proscilutin' attorney.

Amos: You goin' ast me questions now?

Andy: Whut is today?

Amos: Today is-a—whut IS today—today is Sat'day.

Andy: You come pretty near makin' me mad den. Whut do I do fur a livin'?

Amos: You mean whut is you doin' fur livin'?

Andy: Dat's right—whut do I do fur livin'?

Amos: You is lookin' fur a job.

Andy: No-no—I is a lawyer.

Amos: Is you sho' 'nuf?

Andy: I is a lawyer—dat's whut I is.

Amos: Oh, you mean dat's whut I goin' tell Miz Lee.
Andy: I'll do de talkin'—put on yore coat.
Amos: I tell you—I won't say nothin'—we'll jest go on over dere an' I'll let you do all de talkin'.
Andy: You gits me so mad I don' know whut I'se doin'. You ready to go?
Amos: Yeah—I'se ready to go.
(Knock on door.)
Andy: Somebody at de do'. Come in—come in.
Amos: Hello dere, landlord.
Land: Hello, boys—Yere's a note dat jest come fur you boys from Miz Lee, de washwoman.
Andy: Open dat thing up. Whut do it say?
Amos: Lissen to it—it says—thank you boys fur de fried chicken—it wuz jest as tender an' nice as it could be—me an' my husband enjoyed it a lot—signed Miz Lee.
Andy: Dere you go now—see dere. . . . .
Amos: Well, I couldn't help it if she done eat de chicken up—I couldn't help it. . . . .

XV

Amos and Andy found their financial condition very bad and in order to relieve the situation Amos was forced to sell newspapers to raise sufficient funds to enable the boys to eat. Andy has been watching Amos sell the papers and, as the scene opens now, we find the boys on their way home—Amos has just sold his last paper and has 65 cents which represents the day's business.

AMOS: Dis yere ain't bad fur de first day, is it? I done made 65 cents.

ANDY: Now, wait a minute—don't git too frisky yere. All dat 65 cents ain't yourn. We is got to 'vide it.

AMOS: Whut you mean—we got to 'vide it?

ANDY: We is goin' half on ever'thing, ain't we?

AMOS: Yeah—we is goin' half a'right but you tol' me dat if I wanted some money fur myself to go ahaid, make some—so I started sellin' papers.

ANDY: Wait a minute though. Who's idea wuz dat?

AMOS: Whut you mean, who's idea wuz it?

ANDY: Lissen yere, Amos—You ought to know by now dat I is got de brains of a lawyer. In de fust place, de man dat de-ceives de idea, 'cordin' to law—has got de rights to de a-forsaid.

AMOS: I don' know whut you is talkin' 'bout now. 'Splain dat to me.
ANDY: I wuz de one dat had de idea about you sellin' newspapers—so I gits half of ever'thing you makes as long as you is workin' on my idea.
AMOS: I wuz de one dat said dat I could make some money sellin' newspapers.
ANDY: But *I* wuz de one dat tol' you to go ahead. In other words, I suppo'ted yore party, an' 'cordin' to de law, I gits half o' dat 65 cents.
AMOS: I don' care den if you think you ought to have half of it—I'll give it to you.
ANDY: 65—'vided by two. Half o' six is fo'—nobody to carry.
AMOS: Wait a minute yere—wait a minute—do dat again.
ANDY: We is 'vidin' 65 by 2, ain't we? Half o' six is fo'—an' half o' five—is-a—
AMOS: Wait a minute yere. I got 65 cents yere, ain't I?
ANDY: Gimme 35 cents an' I'll call it square.
AMOS: Well, dat's a'right den if you'll do dat. Yere—hold yore hand yere.
ANDY: Wait a minute—don't gimme none o' dem pennies. Gimme dem dimes an' nickels.
AMOS: I ain't got but three dimes.
ANDY: Gimme three dimes an' dat nickel.
AMOS: Yere you is—yere you is.
ANDY: Wait a minute, wait a minute—dis yere's a Canada dime. You keep dis dime an' gimme ten pennies.
AMOS: A'right, I'll take it back.
ANDY: I'se givin' you de best of ever'thing—but I

don' care—dat shows you dat I'se a friend o' yore's.

Amos: I b'lieve I'll git up in de mornin' an' sell papers all day long.

Andy: De thing *I* got do is to git you a job where you kin make mo' money.

Amos: I don't know how I goin' make mo' money —I can't git a job.

Andy: While you is sellin' papers tomorrow, I'll wait at home in case anybody comes after us, I'll be dere. Ain't no use fur both of us to be out at de same time.

Amos: Ain't you goin' sell papers?

Andy: Ain't no use fur me to sell papers—I got git me a JOB somewheres wid a big comp'ny. I'se jest wastin' my time sellin' papers.

Amos: De trouble is though—we got git SOME money in yere so we kin eat on it till we DO git a job.

Andy: Don' worry 'bout me—I'll eat. You jest keep on makin' de money.

Amos: De trouble is—I can't make enough fur both of us, Andy.

Andy: But if you kin live on half o' whut you make, I kin git by on de other half. Don't you worry 'bout me—You jest figure on livin' on half o' whut you make, an' I'll take de other half an', with whut little money I IS got, I kin git by as long as you kin.

Amos: Longer!

Andy: De thing I b'lieve I'll do now is git me sumpin' to eat.

Amos: I'se certainly plen'y hungry, I know dat.

Andy: Well, de thing fur us to do is to go over yere

to dis lunch room an' git sumpin' to eat—dat's whut we better do. Whut is you goin' eat when you git over dere?

AMOS: Well, I ain't got enough money to eat whut I wants to eat 'cause if I got buy papers tomorrow, I can't 'ford to eat nothin' but a hot dog.

ANDY: Dere you go, you see—you don' take care o' yore money—dat's whut de trouble is.

AMOS: I tries to take care of it de best I kin. De trouble is—it jest seems to leave me, dat's whut it do.

ANDY: Yere you is—wid about fifty cents in yore pocket an' I got fo' dollars an' ninety cents an' we both come up yere to Chicago wid de same 'mount o' money. How do you 'count fur dat?

AMOS: Well, I tell you—

ANDY: Shut up!

AMOS: 'Scuse me.

ANDY: Carelessness—nothin' but carelessness—watch yore dollars,—dat's whut I been tellin' you, Amos.

AMOS: I know you is, Andy.

ANDY: If you lissen to me sometime, you'll have a little money.

AMOS: I tries to listen to you. De trouble is though, I have to spend too much money.

ANDY: I'se livin' de same as you is an' I ain't spendin' all o' my money.

AMOS: I know but—

ANDY: Shut up! Carelessness, dat's all 'tis.

AMOS: I wish I COULD save a few dollars—git myself a job or sumpin'. Yere I is up yere in

Chicago—ain't got no money, ain't got no job or nothin'.

ANDY: Don' start cryin' now or I'll bus' you over de haid, dat's whut I'll do.

AMOS: I ain't cryin', Andy—But I'se jest kind of homesick, dat's whut I is.

ANDY: Now, wait a minute. I is jest like a big banker.

AMOS: Whut you mean?

ANDY: I ain't got no feeling fur nobody 'less dey saves dey're money.

AMOS: Well, soon as I git a job, I goin' save some money. I wanted to make enough today to send Ruby Taylor a box o' dem little pep'mint things—cost fifteen cents—pep'mint candy things, but I can't 'ford to do dat.

ANDY: Dere's where yore money goes. Now stop an' an-alrize de sitiation. Dat is jest like throwin' fifteen cents out de window.

AMOS: I know—But she's been nice to us since we'se been yere.

ANDY: Dat ain't nothin'—don't NEVER spend fifteen cents on no gal. Come on, let's git over yere to de res-trant—I got eat.

AMOS: I'll go over dere wid you but I can't spend much money.

ANDY: When I git you home tonight I'm goin' give you some good sound re-vice.

AMOS: Whut I need is a good job, dat's whut I need.

ANDY: If you lissen to me an' do whut I tell you to do, you'll git a job.

AMOS: I know, Andy—but I 'member when we was down in Georgia—you was de one dat wanted me to come up yere wid you—an' you told me dat if we come up yere—to Chicago—dat jobs wuz easy to git. You told me dat people would jest grab us an' put us to work. I hate to be always talkin' 'bout not havin' work but I ain't never been so homesick as I is right now—I'se homesick an' hungry, dat's whut I is.

ANDY: When you talks like dat, Amos, I gits regusted wid you. I didn't BRING you up yere—you paid yore own railroad fare up yere.

AMOS: I know I paid my own railroad fare—now don't git mad wid me, Andy—I'se jest tellin' you how I feel, dat's all.

ANDY: De trouble wid you is—you don' use yore haid. You got a haid, de same as I is.

AMOS: I guess it's all my fault—I don' know. Jest seems like I can't git goin', dat's all.

ANDY: Now, lissen yere—after I finish talkin' to you tonight, if you let whut I tell you soak in yore haid—You'll git out yere in de mornin'—yore li'ble to make $25 tomorrow.

AMOS: I certainly do wish I COULD git out an' make some money. I'se 'shamed to write back home. I told Mamie I'd write her soon as I got up yere.

ANDY: Don't start thinkin' 'bout gals now—come on, let's git on in de lunch room yere.

AMOS: I'se comin'—I'se comin'.

ANDY: Sit up dere at de counter—dat's where we wants to sit.

AMOS: Certainly do smell good in yere, don't it?

ANDY: Sit down dere now. Don't talk so much. Yere come de man.

MAN: Alright, boys—what do you want?

ANDY: Gimme a teabone steak, Mister.

MAN: Teabone steak. Whut for you?

AMOS: How much is yore beans, Mister—baked beans?

MAN: Nice baked beans—fifteen cents.

AMOS: You ain't got no ten cent ones, is you?

MAN: Baked beans are fifteen cents.

AMOS: Well, Mister, I guess you better gimme one o' dem ten cent hamberger san'wiches, will you please, sah.

MAN: (fading out) One-a tea-bone steak—an' one-a hamburger san'wich—comin' up.

ANDY: Wait a minute, Mister—you better smother dat steak o' mine wid onions.

MAN: Onions on the teabone.

AMOS: Andy—I certainly do feel sad tonight.

ANDY: Lissen, Amos—don't git down-hearted—I gonna give you half o' dis steak I got coming—

XVI

Amos and Andy went to a dance. Amos went with Ruby Taylor while Andy's dancing partner was a rather stout girl by the name of Rosie Waite. Everything went along very lovely until Andy danced with Rosie Waite's mother and during this dance Andy's feet were constantly in the way. As we find the boys now they are home after the dance—Andy has just finished soaking his feet in hot water.

AMOS: I certainly is sorry dat dey stepped on yore feets las' night.

ANDY: No mo' dancin' fur me, Amos. I'se re-gusted wid dancin'.

AMOS: Is yore feets very sore now?

ANDY: Is my feets sore? If I had enough money, I'd go to a hospital, dat's whut I'd do.

AMOS: You wuz de one dat told me though that you knew all 'bout dancin'.

ANDY: I STILL knows all 'bout it—but de other peoples is de ones dat don't know.

AMOS: While I wuz dancin' wid Miss Taylor, I looked over at you once—right in de middle o' de dance I saw you stop an' pick up yore foot an' rub it.

ANDY: An' de minute I laid dat dog back down on de floor, she jumped right on it again.

AMOS: Who was dat dat stepped on yore feets—Miss Waite's mama?

ANDY: Miss Waite's mama wid all her weight—an' she is bigger dan Rosie is.
AMOS: I wonder whut make 'em do dat?
ANDY: Well, you know some peoples has a hobby-hoss.
AMOS: Some peoples has whut?
ANDY: Some peoples has a hobby-hoss—some peoples hobby-hoss is fishin'. Somebody else'll have a hobby-hoss shootin' pool—somebody else'll have a hobby-hoss playin' cards. Rosie Waite's mama's hobby-hoss is steppin' on feets.
AMOS: How come you didn't git yore feets out de way?
ANDY: No matter where I'd lay 'em down she wuz right on 'em. Once dere durin' de dance she stepped on dis left dog o' mine an' I hollered "Ow"—an' I picked my left foot up an' started rubbin' it while de music wuz still playin' an' while I wuz rubbin' my left foot, she wuz standin' on my right one.
AMOS: I certainly is sorry though dat you done got yo' feets all bruised up.
ANDY: It jest seemed to me las' night dat dey wuz layin' fur my feets.
AMOS: Well, didn't you have a good time though?
ANDY: I didn't have no good time. My feets hurt me too bad.
AMOS: When we went over to Rosie Waite's house though an' had de food after de dance wuz over—dat wuz nice.
ANDY: Dat's when my feets started givin' me mo' trouble.
AMOS: How come yore feets hurt you over dere?
ANDY: Well, you 'member dat Rosie Waite's mama

Amos: While I was dancin' wid Miss Taylor, I looked over at you once—right in de middle o' de dance I saw you stop an' pick up yore foot an' rub it.

Andy: An' de minute I laid dat dog back down on de floor, Rosie Waite's mama jumped right on it again.

sat at de end o' de table—you wuz on one side o' her—an' I wuz right across from you.
AMOS: I 'members dat a'right. She wuz at de end o' de table an' you wuz sittin' at de right o' her—an' I was right across from you.
ANDY: Well, dey have a button under de rug dat rings a bell out in de kitchen or somewheres dat brings de cook in an' about ev'vy thirty seconds Rosie's mama would say 'de bell wuzn't workin'.' No wonder it wuzn't workin'—she wuzn't steppin' on de bells—she wuz steppin' on my foot.
AMOS: You certainly did have a time of it at de dance las' night, I know dat.
ANDY: De trouble is—ev'vy time I wuz waltzin', somebody else wuz fox-trottin'.
AMOS: I certainly do likes Miss Taylor—she tol' me dat I wuz a good dancer an' I told her dat she wuz a good dancer too.
ANDY: De fust thing you know, you goin' be fallin' in love wid dat gal.
AMOS: I ain't goin' fall in love wid nobody.
ANDY: Remember now, boy, you don' wants to start no love-nest up yere.
AMOS: I got git me a job—dat's de fust thing I got do.
ANDY: De thing YOU got do is to git out an' look fur work an' stop hangin' 'round wid dese boys 'round town yere wastin' time.
AMOS: I done looked fur work—de only trouble is, I can't find none. I'se willin' to do anything in de world if I jest kin git some work.
ANDY: I could give you a little 'zamination to find out whut kind o' work you kin qualifly fur.

AMOS: Whut kind o' fly?
ANDY: Lissen yere, son—when dey puts you to work now-a-days, dey always gives you a 'zamination—den 'cordin' to yore qualifly-lations, you gits de job.
AMOS: I don' know whut all dat means—'splain dat to me, will you Andy?
ANDY: Well now lissen—I'll give you a 'zamination.
AMOS: Whut you mean?
ANDY: I'll be de 'ployER an' you be de 'ployEE—an' I'll ast you de questions.
AMOS: Whut you wants to do is to play—play a game, is dat whut you wants to do?
ANDY: No, no—now lissen—you is lookin' fur work—you is 'ployEE, an' I is de owner of a big comp'ny.
AMOS: I b'lieve you'se done gone crazy, Andy.
ANDY: No, no, now lissen—you is got qualifly.
AMOS: I is?
ANDY: An' I is goin' qualifly you.
AMOS: You ain't goin' hurt me, is you?
ANDY: No, no—all I goin' do is to ast you some questions to see whut 'partment to put you in. Now, I owns a big fac'try. I makes ever'thing.
AMOS: I wish you owned a lunch room.
ANDY: Now, wait a minute—I'm goin' ast you some questions. Now, you is jest walked into my office. Whut is de fust thing you would say when you see me yere?
AMOS: I'd say—"How is you feets gittin' along?"
ANDY: No, no—furgit about de feet.
AMOS: Is dey done stopped hurtin'?
ANDY: No, no, now lissen—jest 'magine dat you is

in de man's office an' I is de man. De man say-a—"Good mornin', whut are YOU doin' yere?" Whut would YOU say?

AMOS: I'd say: "Dis yere's my room, dis yere's where I sleep."

ANDY: No, no, you is in de man's office. De man says "sit down"—den he starts astin' you questions. Now, yere comes de 'zamination.

AMOS: Go ahaid, start de 'zamination.

ANDY: Young man, whut is yore name?

AMOS: My name is Amos Jones.

ANDY: Where is you from, Amos Jones?

AMOS: I'se from Georgia right near Atlanta.

ANDY: Mr. Jones-a—befo' I kin put you to work I'se got see if you know anything. How much is five an' ten?

AMOS: You mean de five an' ten cent sto'?

ANDY: No, no, I mean de grand total.

AMOS: Oh, dat's diff'ent.

ANDY: You give up?

AMOS: I give up.

ANDY: Now, wait a minute. If you acted like dat, de man would put you to work in de boiler room. Whut you wants to be is a exe*cu*tive.

AMOS: Dat's whut I wants to be, huh?

ANDY: I'll ast you some mo'. Mr. Jones, do you think dat you could handle de third floor o' de fac'try?

AMOS: Whut you want me to do—sweep it up?

ANDY: No, no, de man don' want you to sweep de floor—de man's givin' you a big job yere.

AMOS: Whut mus' I tell him—I kin do it?

ANDY: Tell him you kin do anything—den when he finds out you can't do it, he'll fire you.

AMOS: Ain't no use to ast me no more questions like dat, Andy. I don' want a big job—all I wants to do is to start wid a little job an' den work myself up.

ANDY: Wait a minute yere now—I'se givin' you a good job. You is gittin' a 'zamination now.

AMOS: I know, but I'se gittin' all mixed up on it.

ANDY: I'm goin' ast you one question yere dat ever'thing 'pends on. Answer dis question an' de job is yourn.

AMOS: Go ahead, ast me.

ANDY: Whut is fifteen re-vided by three?

AMOS: Fifteen re-vided by three is ten.

ANDY: O. K. YOU gits de job. Dat's de way to do de thing. I didn't think you wuz goin' git dat las' one.

AMOS: De trouble is yere though—I wants a job dat dey ain't goin' ast me so many questions at fust till I git used to it.

ANDY: De trouble wid you is, you is hangin' 'round wid dese boys 'round town yere till you'se wastin' all yore time, dat's whut you'se doin'.

AMOS: De only one dat I goes wid at all is Sylvester. He's a *good* boy.

ANDY: Sylvester ain't no good. All he is tryin' to do is to git you in trouble.

AMOS: Sylvester's a good boy though, Andy.

ANDY: Dis boy Sylvester—I is done looked him over an' if anybody knows men, *I* is de one dat knows him an' I is done come to de 'clusion dat he ain't NO good.

AMOS: I ain't knowed him but a short time but I bet-cha he'd give us de shirt off his back.

ANDY: De way I got it figured out, he'd TAKE de shirt off yore back. I don' want you to hang around wid dat guy no mo'.
AMOS: You means you don' want me to have no mo' to do wid him?
ANDY: Let him alone.
AMOS: I certainly do hates to fall out wid Sylvester 'cause I likes him. Ever'body in town likes him dat I knows.
ANDY: Now, you do whut I tell you—let him alone—he ain't no good.
AMOS: I'll do whut you say a'right—de only thing is—
(Knock at door.)
ANDY: Wait a minute—dere's somebody at de do'—Come in. Well—Sylvester.
SYL: Hello, Mr. Amos—Hello, Mr. Andy.
AMOS: Hello, Sylvester—how is you?
SYL: I'se a'right, thank you. I got some good news fur you gent'mens.
ANDY: Whut is dat?
SYL: Dey is buildin' a gymnasium down here on de South side an' I got you boys a job down dere tomorrow if you want it startin' tomorrow.
AMOS: Is you done done dat, sho' 'nuf, Sylvester?
ANDY: Well—dat sounds pretty good.
SYL: De man say he'll pay you pretty good money an' he wants you to come right on down dere now an' talk to him.
ANDY: Git yore hat, Amos.
AMOS: I'se ready to go right now. Come on—let's go down dere an' see him.
SYL: I tol' him dat you wuz friends o' mine an' he say he'll put you to work right away.

ANDY: Funny thing, Sylvester, how things works out. I wuz jest tellin' Amos whut a good boy you wuz—an' den all of a sudden you knocked on de do' an' in you walked—funny thing 'bout dat—funny 'bout dat. . . . .

XVII

Through the efforts of Sylvester, Amos and Andy get the job in the gymnasium which is under construction. As we find the two boys now, they are on their way home after their first day of work.

AMOS: I kind of glad de work is over fur today. Come on, let's git on home, Andy.
ANDY: I'se glad de work is over too. De trouble is wid dat work, it keeps me on my feets too much.
AMOS: Is yore feets givin' you any trouble now?
ANDY: Boy, dey is on fire, dat's whut dey is.
AMOS: I made a lot o' mistakes down dere today. I didn't know whut dem mens was talkin' 'bout.
ANDY: De trouble is wid you—you ain't got de brains dat I is got. If I had my way down dere, I'd tear down dat gymnasium an' build 'em another one.
AMOS: I thought de thing looked pretty good to me.
ANDY: Dat thing is goin' be a *cheap* gymnasium. Ain't even goin' have no carpet on de flo'.
AMOS: After dey gits it fixed up though, it's goin' be pretty, I b'lieve. Dey goin' start paintin' down dere pretty soon.
ANDY: De trouble is wid it—de people dat is buildin' de thing down dere—dey ain't got de right idea,

an' if I stay down dere long enough, I'll be foreman.

Amos: I'se glad enough to work down dere myself. How much is dey payin' us now? Dey'se givin' us twenty dollers a week, ain't dey?

Andy: Twenty dollers a week. Me—a big bizness man like I is gittin' twenty dollers a week. Dat's a dis-regrace.

Amos: Dat's better dan gittin' nothin' though.

Andy: De way I feels 'bout it—I'd ruther see de two of us live on whut you make dan to have a man wid my 'bility workin' fur twenty dollers a week. Don't never tell nobody I work fur dat.

Amos: I'se proud to be workin' fur dat much money. Dat's good money. Dat's more money dan we made down in Atlanta.

Andy: But we is in Chicago now. 'Spose I was in de notion o' gittin' a automobile. Dat wouldn't pay fur de gas an' oil.

Amos: Ain't no use to think 'bout gittin' a automobile now though.

Andy: De thing I mus' do is to go to de boss an' tell him dat I'se a smart man.

Amos: I don't guess de boss thinks I got any sense.

Andy: I told him today dat you was a dumbbell.

Amos: I tell you whut I'd LIKE to do—I'd like to git a steady job wid dat comp'ny—so after dey gits dis gymnasium finished, I won't be out o' work.

Andy: De thing I is fixin' to do yere is open up some kind o' bizness in Chicago.

Amos: We ain't got no money to go in no bizness.

Andy: Lemme see yere—whut kind o' bizness I could open up. I could open up a garage fixin' automobiles. De trouble is, you don' know nothin' 'bout 'em.

AMOS: I don' know much about automobiles. Maybe if you think o' sumpin' else I might be able to do it. I could wash automobiles.

ANDY: I could open up a fillin' station.

AMOS: De only trouble is—we ain't got nothin' to fill 'em wid. You mean sell gasoline?

ANDY: I could open up a fillin' station an' run some o' dese big oil comp'nies out o' bizness.

AMOS: Dat's goin' take a lot o' money to do sumpin' like dat though, ain't it?

ANDY: De way I figures de thing out, I kin git a fillin' station an' have ever'thing running by 'lectricity.

AMOS: Whut you mean have ever'thing runnin' by 'lectricity?

ANDY: Well, I kin sit down on de inside in a big chair and when de peoples come up to git de gasoline, all dey is got do is to take de hose an' put it in de gas tank an' dey kin holler in at me—how much gasoline dey wants an' I press a button an' de gasoline come right on out. Den dey brings me de money, so you see I saves all my strength an' brains to think.

AMOS: 'Spose de people wants some water though to put in de front o' de automobile.

ANDY: Dey knows where de hose is.

AMOS: Well, dat might work out a'right. De only trouble is—it's goin' take a lot o' money to go into anything like dat.

ANDY: Lemme figure up yere now—whut else I kin do to make some money?

AMOS: We could go in de dairy bizness but we ain't got no cows, is we?

ANDY: Wait a minute—don't *you* think—lemme do de thinkin'—you gits me mixed up when YOU think.

AMOS: You go ahaid den—I'll lissen to you.

ANDY: I got sit down in a dark room by myself an' con-sonlate—put all de lights out.

AMOS: You goin' con-sonlate in a room by yoreself?

ANDY: My brain is diff'ent from yore's, Amos. I'se got be like de big mens dat has de private office. Dat's whut I ought to have. I ain't got no bizness livin' in de same room wid you.

AMOS: Well, if you wants me to when you wants to con-sonlate, I'll git out an' walk up an' down de street till you finish.

ANDY: De trouble is—whut I need is capital. If I had two—three hund'ed dollers I could turn dis town upside down.

AMOS: Well, if we git together an' save up our money, we ought to have two-three hund'ed dollers by next Chrismus.

ANDY: Whut I got do is git goin' yere befo' Chrismus comes 'round. I tell you whut—I might open a second hand clothin' sto'—I might do dat.

AMOS: Where you goin' git de clothes to sell?

ANDY: De clothes? Yeah, dat makes it bad—I could start out sellin' YORE clothes.

AMOS: Don' sell none o' mine—I ain't got many—don' sell dem.

ANDY: Dere you go now—see—holdin' me back. I'se tryin' to get a start yere an' you don' wants to help me.

AMOS: I wants to help you a'right but I don' want

you to sell my clothes. How is I goin' git out o' de house?

ANDY: I kin see dat I is got git in a dark room an' consonlate, dat's whut I got do.

AMOS: Ruby Taylor's papa might tell us how we kin make some money.

ANDY: I know how to make it. All I got do is to git started, dat's all. I could open up a bus-line—de trouble is dere though, I ain't got no busses.

AMOS: Yeah—you ought to have a bus if you goin' open up a bus line.

ANDY: If I had a taxi-cab, I could open up a taxi-cab comp'ny.

AMOS: Sylvester was tellin' me dat a lot o' de boys is got taxi-cabs.

ANDY: If I could buy a automobile on credit, I might start a taxi comp'ny an' run de rest o' dese yere taxi comp'nies out o' bizness.

AMOS: Dat might be a way to make a lot o' money. Who would drive de thing, me or you?

ANDY: You could drive de thing an' I could git myself a seat up in front an' go long wid you to see dat ever'thing work a'right.

AMOS: I wish we WOULD git in some kind o' bizness yere 'cause de way we is goin' now, we ain't doin' much.

ANDY: Dat's yore fault. I thinks o' things fur you to do but you don't do 'em.

AMOS: Well, we got a job down dere now. If we kin keep goin' on dat we kin git by.

ANDY: De thing fur you to do now is when you git yore money, is to take it right down to de bank an' have it compounded—'vest de principal on de int'rest—den you is got a su'plus dat you kin work on.

AMOS: Ain't no two ways 'bout dat—if we could do dat.

ANDY: We gits paid Sat'day—now dat's tomorrow.

AMOS: De only trouble, I done borrowed two dollers on my sal'ry already. Dey is gonna 'duck dat, ain't dey?

ANDY: You kin still have dat compounded though. Git de 'crued int'rest comin' in—dat's whut you got do.

AMOS: You better handle de money of it—'bout all dem things you jest talkin' 'bout.

ANDY: How much money will you have comin' tomorrow?

AMOS: Well, I done borrowed two dollers on my sal'ry an' it's a fella somewheres 'round yere dat has fits. I give him three dollers on dose fits.

ANDY: Whut kind o' fits?

AMOS: I guess he jest has straight fits. De fella's name is Benny. De man ast me fur three dollars fur sick Benny's fits.

ANDY: Benny's fits. Wait a minute yere—boy, you gits me madder an' madder. Dat's benefits.

AMOS: Dat's whut I say—dat's Benny's fits.

ANDY: Dey is fur YORE benefits.

AMOS: No, no, I don't have any fits—Benny has 'em. Cost me three dollers ev'vy quarter.

ANDY: Three dollers ev'vy quarter?

AMOS: I figured dat out—dats three dollers an' a quarter, ain't it?

ANDY: Three dollers ev'vy quarter—three dollers an' twen'y-five cents.

Amos: De man says he'd be 'round again in three months. I give him three dollers on my sal'ry—but he didn't take de quarter.
Andy: How much do de thing pay?
Amos: Well, I don't git nothin' till Benny gits one o' dem fits—den I gits 'leven dollers a week.
Andy: You gits 'leven dollers a week. Now lissen—dat ain't got nuthin' to do wid Benny—dat's you. If you gits sick, you gits 'leven dollers a week—dat's whut dat thing is.
Amos: Oh, I'SE de one dat's got git sick, huh?
Andy: You done paid three dollers fur dat an' done borrowed two dollers on yore salary—'cordin' to dat, you draws 'bout $1.35 tomorrow.
Amos: Is dat all I gits tomorrow—a doller an' thirty-five cents?
Andy: Dat's all you git—$1.35. I could take dat to de bank an' put dat up as cor-rat-ral an' git de int'rest comin' in—
Amos: Wait a minute though—how is I goin' eat over Sunday?
Andy: Dat IS right—you got eat, ain't you? Could you make three bananas las' you over Sunday?
Amos: Dey would fill me up but dey wouldn't do me no good. I got git some cigarettes too.
Andy: You kin find enough stumps layin' 'round de room.
Amos: I done smoked all dem stumps.
Andy: A'right den—you don't wants to co-opulate wid me—take de $1.35 an' spend it.
Amos: I wants to co-opulate wid you.
Andy: I tell you whut we'll do—we'll take yore $1.35 an' me 'n' you will eat on dat over Sunday.

Amos: Whut you goin' do wid yore salary?
Andy: I better put dat in de bank. You see, I ain't got no sick benefits so I'se got re-teck myself case sumpin' happens.
Amos: Well, I don't care—we'll do whutever you say. Yere we is home—come on, let's git in de house.
Andy: Yeah—I wants to git in de room an' turn out de lights an' con-sonlate—maybe I'll think of a better idea dan dat.

XVIII

Amos and Andy received their pay envelope and immediately started for home. They have only worked two days this week and have very little money. As we find them now, they are about a half a block from home.

AMOS: I certainly is glad dat today is Sat'day.
ANDY: I is goin' stay in bed tomorrow an' rest up.
AMOS: How much money did you git?
ANDY: I done told you once I got seven dollers an' thirty-three cents.
AMOS: I got more den I thought I wuz goin' git. You know I borrowed two dollers on my sal'ry an' den I paid out three dollers fur dat sick benefits—I didn't git but two dollers and thirty-three cents.
ANDY: Well, let's git on home an' lay down an' rest—dat's whut I wants to do. If dem mens is goin' run me 'round ev'vy day like dey did today, I goin' quit.
AMOS: We better hold on to dat job though till we kin git another one.
ANDY: Soon as I gits about thirty-five dollers, I goin' tell dat man he kin have his job. Den I'll be inrependent.
AMOS: I don' believe I'll quit till I git another one.
ANDY: Well, come on—let's git on in de house yere

so I kin take off my shoes. My dogs is barkin *right* now.

Amos: We got pay de lan'lord sumpin' on de rent—don't furgit 'bout dat.

Andy: Let's git on in de house yere, boy.

Amos: Wait a minute yere—I wants to stop an' see if I got any mail.

Andy: Who you goin' hear from? Git on back in de room dere.

Amos: Wait a minute Andy—yere's a letter yere from Atlanta!

Andy: How come dey know you was stayin' yere?

Amos: I furgot to tell you—I writ Mamie a letter de other day an' told her where to write me.

Andy: Come on—git back in de room. De trouble wid you is—you always talkin' 'bout gals—thinkin' 'bout 'em all de time.

Amos: Well, when I left Atlanta, I tol' Mamie I wuz gonna write her soon as I got up yere.

Andy: Half de time yore thinkin' 'bout Mamie an' de other half, you'se thinkin' 'bout dis gal Ruby Taylor—you ain't never goin' be a bizness man.

Amos: I told Ruby Taylor 'bout Mamie. I told her dat me 'n' Mamie is done been sweethearts ever since we wuz little children runnin' 'round together.

Andy: I bet-cha dat made Ruby mad.

Amos: No it didn't. Ruby say dat she wuz goin' write Mamie a letter an' 'vite her up yere to Chicago—she say dat she kin stay over at Ruby's house.

Andy: You ain't fallin' in love wid none o' dese gals, is you?

Amos: Well, I done always been in love wid Mamie.

ANDY: Git out o' dat chair dere. Lemme sit down dere an' take my shoes off. You know I always sits in de rockin' chair.

AMOS: Go ahaid—sit down dere—I'll sit yere on de bed.

ANDY: An' don' sit on dat bed dere—'cause after I git my shoes off I'se comin' over der an' stretch out.

AMOS: I'll stand up yere den till you takes yore shoes off. We ought to git another chair in de room yere—dat's whut we ought to do.

ANDY: Read me whut Mamie say.

AMOS: Wait a minute—lemme git de letter open yere.

ANDY: Go ahaid—read it—wait a minute, lemme git on de bed yere fust.

AMOS: She say yere—she starts out—she say: "Dear Amos—I'se jest got yore letter an' I is glad to know dat you got to Chicago alright."

ANDY: Now, dat's a dumb thing fur her to be writin' up yere. Go ahaid—read on dere, boy.

AMOS: She say-a—"I hope you do not have no trouble findin' work—an' I hope dat dey will grab you an' give you a job like Andy told you dey would."

ANDY: Now, wait a minute. Tell dat gal to keep her mouth shut 'bout me.

AMOS: She don't mean no harm 'bout it. She's just writin' 'bout it.

ANDY: She is always shootin' her mouth 'round 'bout sumpin' dat *I* say.

AMOS: I ain't goin' read you no mo' if you goin' git mad wid her.

ANDY: All she got do is to leave me out of it.

Amos: Well, don't git mad wid Mamie.
Andy: Whut else do she say?
Amos: She say yere—"some of de boys dat went up North to git work is done come back home. Two of de boys dat jest got back today told papa dat dey lost 35 pounds apiece on account o' not eatin'."
Andy: Dem boys—dey ain't got no sense.
Amos: Den she say yere—I want you to take care o' yo'self an' git plen'y to eat.
Andy: Write her back an' tell her you is eatin' like a hoss.
Amos: De nex' part o' her letter yere is kind of pussonel—ain't no use to read you dat.
Andy: You ain't goin' hold nothin' out on me, is you?
Amos: I ain't holdin' nothin' out on you—dis yere is jest a little stuff though dat I ain't tol' nobody 'bout.
Andy: Whut do it say? Read me ever'thing dat's in dere.
Amos: Well, she say yere—"I is got yore pitcher on de b-u-r-o-e"—whut is dat?
Andy: Dat's a burro—dat's on a mule—maybe she's got yore pitcher tied around a donkey's neck.
Amos: Wait a minute—dat ain't whut she means—dat's b-u-r—dat's bureau, dat's whut dat is.
Andy: Whut do it say again?
Amos: She say—"I is got yore pitcher on de bureau an' it is de las' thing I see at night an' de fust thing I see in de mornin'."
Andy: Dat makes me sick—an' if she look at it long enough, she'll git sick too.

Amos: Wait a minute yere now, Andy—you ast me to read you de letter. Don't git mad now.

Andy: I ain't gittin' mad—I jest hate dis love stuff, dat's all—dat's all I hears from you.

Amos: Den she say yere—"you know, Amos, we is been goin' together since we wuz little chillun an' dis is de fust time we is been away from each other." Dat certainly was sweet o' her to say dat, wuzn't it?

Andy: Ain't nothin' sweet 'bout it.

Amos: Den she say yere—"I told papa dis mornin' dat his ole sayin' wuz right—dat you never miss de water till de well runs dry."

Andy: De mo' I heah, de mo' re-gusted I gits.

Amos: Den she say—"write to me often 'cause I is always thinkin' of you. Tell Andy 'hello'."

Andy: I don' even wants to hear it.

Amos: She jest says "hello" to you, dat's all.

Andy: I don' want nobody helloin' me.

Amos: Den she say—"lots o' love—yore sweetheart,—Mamie."

Andy: Now listen yere—if you come up yere to work, let's work. Furgit about dese gals.

Amos: Well, I'se tendin' to de work. De only thing—I can't help gittin' a letter now an' den.

Andy: De trouble is—you don't think o' nothin' but gals. Think o' some way we kin make money like I do. De fust thing you done when we got to town yere is meet dis yere gal Ruby Taylor—den you gits a long love letter from Mamie.

Amos: De best thing fur me to do is not to read you any mo' o' my letters, dat's whut.

Andy: I don't care if you read 'em to me or not. De thing we got do is be bizness men.

Amos: I'se willin' to do anything I kin.
Andy: Git me a pencil an' a piece o' paper dere.
Amos: Whut you goin' do—start figgerin'?
Andy: Don't ast so many questions, Amos—do whut I tell you to do. Now, gimme sumpin' I kin write on—han' me dat book over dere.
Amos: Maybe you kin write on top o' dis magazine—kin you do dat?
Andy: Dat's a'right—hand it yere. Yere I is—all worn out—yet no matter how tired I gits, I'se always figgerin'. I guess I'll die figgerin'.
Amos: If we don't keep dis job dat we got, both of us goin' die figgerin' out how to make a livin', I know dat.
Andy: I ain't worried 'bout myself—YOU is de one I is worried 'bout. Far as *I* is 'cerned I kin go out yere an' make money any time I wants to.
Amos: Why don't you do dat? Don't you wants to make money?
Andy: I'se got look after you, ain't I?
Amos: No, don't worry 'bout me—you go ahaid, make some money fur yoreself if you wants to.
Andy: Well, I was de one dat told you to come on up yere an' I feels de 'sponsibility.
Amos: Well, whut is you figgerin' dere now?
Andy: How much money did YOU git?
Amos: I got two dollers and thirty-three cents—dat's all de money dat I got in de envelope. How much did you git?
Andy: Dat ain't none o' yore bizness but I'll tell you—I got seven dollers and thirty-three cents.
Amos: Well, whut is you goin' figure out dere now?
Andy: I'm tryin' to figure out if we is got enough money to go in bizness. I'se plen'y tired yere

too. Yere I is workin' while my brain is so tired I can't even keep my eyes open.

AMOS: Whut is you figgerin'?

ANDY: Lemme see yere now—(getting sleepy) two dollers an' thirty-three cents is whut *you* got (yawns)—an' I got—well, I won't count mine.

AMOS: Kin I help you?

ANDY: Keep quiet a minute now—lemme close my eyes—see if I kin git de answer.

AMOS: You goin' close yore eyes an' try an' see it, huh?

ANDY: Wait a minute now—I'll close my eyes an' consonlate. Keep quiet now,—wait a minute——

AMOS: Do you see it yet?

ANDY: (snores)

AMOS: Well I be doggoned—he done gone to sleep. When dat boy consonlates, he consonlates.

XIX

Amos and Andy were invited over to Ruby Taylor's home for dinner. Both boys were treated to one of the finest meals they have eaten since their arrival in Chicago. They also had an opportunity of meeting Ruby Taylor's father who is a large building contractor on the South Side of Chicago. Amos did several things which met with Andy's disapproval and as the scene opens now we find the two boys just after leaving Ruby Taylor's home.

AMOS: Dat certainly wuz a good meal we had but I wuz scared to death de whole time I wuz dere.

ANDY: You 'barrassed me ev'vy time you opened yore mouth.

AMOS: But I wuz doin' de best I could dere. I didn't know dat I wuz 'barrasin' you. I wuz scared.

ANDY: In de fust place when Ruby's papa ast you how you liked yore steak, you said "Thick."

AMOS: I DO like thick steaks. De trouble is, I never gits none.

ANDY: Dat wuzn't whut de ole man wuz talkin' 'bout.

AMOS: Well—he ast me how I like my steak an' I told him "thick"—dat's all I said.

ANDY: Den another thing—I ain't never seed nobody eat so much wid a knife like you did.

Amos: I used my fork part o' de time.

Andy: Den you had to knock de glass o' water over an' spill it all over ever'thing.

Amos: Dat wuz because I wuz nervous. I wuz so scared dere dat I knocked de water over, I guess.

Andy: I reckon Ruby's ole man thinks we is both crazy. I wuz 'barrassed, I wuz.

Amos: Well, I don't see where I done ever'thing so wrong. I tried to do ever'thing I could dat I knew 'bout.

Andy: Why didn't you use de napkin dat dey give you instead o' puttin' out dat handke'chief you had?

Amos: Well, I kind of felt my face gittin' greasy from eatin' dat steak an' dat napkin dat I had had pretty little flowers all over it—I didn't wants to mess dat thing all up.

Andy: De way you acted, I'se re-gusted wid you.

Amos: Dey said though dat dey wanted us to come over dere again an' eat again.

Andy: When dey brought dem biscuits in dere, instead o' you takin' one biscuit like you ought to, you took fo' biscuits at one time.

Amos: Well, de fust time dey brought 'em round I didn't take but one, an' dey didn't bring 'em out no more till I was 'bout starved to death fur some of 'em—so I said—de next time dey come 'round, I goin' git myself a mess o' dem things.

Andy: You ain't supposed to be a heavy eater when you go out like dat. You is supposed to nibble on de food.

Amos: De trouble is—dey don't set nothin' down on

de table—de cook brings it in an' you git a little dab of it an' den dey takes it out in de kitchen again.

ANDY: Dat's whut you call high eatin'—like dat. Dat's high class eatin'.

AMOS: I wants to have de stuff sittin' on de table so I kin git to it when I'se hungry—dat's whut I want. Dat was a nice dinner though. I ain't never seed so many knifes an' forks on one table. I had seven kinds o' spoons dere—I didn't know WHUT to do wid dem things.

ANDY: De only trouble wuz—dey had all dem flowers in de middle o' de table dere an' I couldn't git yore eye—I couldn't look over dem flowers.

AMOS: Dey was a lot o' flowers in de middle o' de table, wuzn't dey?

ANDY: Seems to me, wid all de room dat man's got 'round dere, he ought to find some place fur dem flowers widout sittin' 'em in de middle o' de table when we is tryin' to eat.

AMOS: If dey'd take dem flowers off de table, dey'd have room to set some o' dem veg'tables down.

ANDY: De trouble is—dey had too much stuff on dat table dat didn't mean nothin'.

AMOS: Dem two candles dat dey had on dere—dey didn't give a bit o' light.

ANDY: Yeah, but you didn't have to tell 'em 'bout it—dat's whut made me mad—you told her papa dat you b'lieved you could see jest as well widout dem candles, if dey wanted to save 'spenses.

AMOS: Well, de way I thought—dem was pretty candles. I thought I would save 'em some money. Dey wasn't givin' a bit o' light over my way.

ANDY: Another thing—when ole man Taylor ast you if you would like to have a demi-tassle, you told him dat you never wear 'em in de spring o' de year.

AMOS: I didn't even know what a demi-tassle wuz—I don't even know now, whut did you tell him when he ast you?

ANDY: I told him no, dat *I* had one. He ain't got know where I keep it or anything—he ain't got know all my bizness—I jest told him dat I had one.

AMOS: Funny way dey acted 'bout de coffee—Ruby Taylor got some an' her papa got some but dey didn't give us none.

ANDY: Dat was kind of cheap, I thought.

AMOS: De dinner was a'right though.

ANDY: When dey served dem little bowls dat you wash yore hands in, boy, you certainly did go to it. How come you roll up yore sleeves when you wash yore hands at de table like dat?

AMOS: My wrists wuz dirty—I saw Ruby an' her papa stickin' dey're hands in de water.

ANDY: Den instead o' lettin' ever'thing alone, you had to git up an' say dat you would empty out de dirty water.

AMOS: Well, I thought dat I'd save dem de trouble o' gettin' up an' throwin' it out—de trouble is, dey didn't give us no soap dere, did dey?

ANDY: Den when de old man passed seegars, you like to choked to death on yourn.

AMOS: I never did like to smoke seegars.

ANDY: I tol' you to keep dat seegar in yore pocket

an' give it to me when you got on de outside.
AMOS: Ruby Taylor certainly was sweet tonight though, wuzn't she? She certainly did look sweet in dat red dress an' wid dat ribbon 'round her hair—she was plen'y sweet.
ANDY: If you'd marry Ruby Taylor, we'd both be millionaires.
AMOS: I ain't thinkin' 'bout marryin' Ruby Taylor—I got a gal. I told Ruby I had one too.
ANDY: De thing dat made me re-gusted wid you wuz when we sit down in dat big room after supper an' we started talkin' bizness wid her papa.
AMOS: De trouble is—he wuz talkin' 'bout a lot o' things dat I didn't know nothin' 'bout.
ANDY: You didn't know nothin' 'bout nothin'.
AMOS: Whut DID he say—I never did figger out whut he wuz talkin' 'bout.
ANDY: He was talkin' 'bout politics dere fur a long time.
AMOS: I never *did* know none o' dem mens dat he was talkin' 'bout.
ANDY: I re-cussed it wid him though. Any time dat he want to re-cuss politics, I re-cussed 'em.
AMOS: You wuz certainly talkin' to him dere fur a long time.
ANDY: You heard whut I tol' him.
AMOS: Whut DID you tell him—I didn't hear it. I wuz talkin' to Ruby Taylor 'bout dat time.
ANDY: I used some big words dere dat knocked him off his feet.
AMOS: Whut did you say?
ANDY: He say dat he didn't think dat Coolidge would run again.

Amos: Run from whut?
Andy: Run fur de President.
Amos: I thought Coolidge was de President. Whut President is he runnin' fur?
Andy: No, no—run fur dis relection.
Amos: Well, what wuz de big word dat you used?
Andy: Lemme see-whut wuz dat big word?—I can't think of it right now—anyway, after I said dat word, de ole man say "I don't understand whut you is talkin' 'bout."
Amos: He didn't say nothin' to you 'bout givin' you a job, did he?
Andy: I told him dat I would drop down an' look some of his buildin's over.
Amos: Whut you goin' look 'em over fur?
Andy: I told him I might 'sider buyin' one o' his buildin's.
Amos: You ain't got no money—how you goin' buy a buildin'—you ain't got enough money to live on, much less talkin' 'bout buyin' a buildin'.
Andy: Well he ain't got know dat. I ast him—I say-a—how much is de buildin's worth?
Amos: Whut did he say to you?
Andy: He said some big number.
Amos: Whutever he said, it wuz too big fur you—I know dat.
Andy: Don't git sarcrastic now. You know I kin handle figgers.
Amos: You kin handle figgers a'right but you ain't got no money to handle, I know dat much.
Andy: De thin' we is got do is to move out o' dat room we is in an' live somewheres dat I kin 'vite some big men over like dat to supper.

Amos: De trouble is—we ain't got enough money to buy a dinner like dat fur nobody.

Andy: De thing we got do is to git in some kind o' bizness so we kin work fur ourselves.

Amos: Whut kind o' bizness is we goin' git in?

Andy: I been tellin' you—if we kin git a second hand automobile an' make a taxicab out of it, dat's de thing to do.

Amos: De trouble is though is to find dat second hand car. Whut kind o' car would you buy?

Andy: Well, lemme see——

Amos: Yo' know-a—if you git a closed car, dey cost almost twice as much as a open car cost.

Andy: You is right 'bout dat, a'right.

Amos: I was talkin' to Sylvester today an' he say dat he knows where we kin git a open car—but it ain't got no top on it.

Andy: Ain't got no top on it, huh?

Amos: He say dat it's in good shape—got tires on it an' ever'thing.

Andy: How much do de thing cost?

Amos: He say it don't cost much an' we kin buy it on time.

Andy: Well, dat sounds pretty good.

Amos: He say we might be able to git it widout payin' anything down on it.

Andy: But it ain't got no top on it, huh?

Amos: No, he say it ain't got no top on it—dat's de trouble.

Andy: Wait a minute—I got a idea.

Amos: Whut is it, whut is it—'splain it to me.

Andy: We kin start sumpin' new—be diff'ent dan anything else in de country—we kin clean up a fortune—make barrels o' money—be million-

aires—have de biggest comp'ny in de world.
AMOS: Wait a minute—wait a minute—'splain dat to me—How we goin' do it?
ANDY: You say de car ain't got no top on it?
AMOS: Dat's de trouble wid it—it ain't got no top on it—but we kin git de car on time.
ANDY: We'll buy dat automobile an' start up a comp'ny called de Fresh Air Taxi Comp'ny.
AMOS: Boy, dat's a idea—Um—um—de Fresh Air Comp'ny—Um-um.

XX

Amos and Andy were paid today and after reaching home they decided to cook supper. During supper Ed and Charlie, the boys who room upstairs, dropped in to say "hello" but only stayed a few moments. As we find Amos and Andy now—they are in their room—dinner is over—Andy is doing a little heavy thinking while Amos is washing the dishes.

AMOS: Don't furgit now—you goin' wash de dishes de nex' time—I ain't goin' wash 'em all de time.
ANDY: Ain't I sittin' yere workin' de same as you is? I'se figgerin' out yere how we goin' make a lot o' money.
AMOS: I know—but I has to wash de dishes all de time. I wants to tell you sumpin' now. I ain't goin' do but half de work around yere—you is gittin' lazy, dat's whut you'se gittin'.
ANDY: Wait a minute yere. Ain't I thinkin' all de time?
AMOS: But it don't mean nothin'. You ain't thinkin' 'bout nothin' dat's done us no good.
ANDY: Look yere now whut I'se done figgered out. Come over yere an' sit down a minute. Un-lax now—un-lax.
AMOS: Whut is you got figgered out yere now?
ANDY: We is goin' down Monday an' see dis automobile dat de man is got fur sale. If we buy de

automobile, we kin start de Fresh Air Taxicab Comp'ny, an' de fust thing you know, both of us'll be rich.

AMOS: Well, whut is dat got do wid you washin' de dishes? Can't you wash de dishes some time jest de same?

ANDY: Now, don't git e'cited Amos. De trouble wid you is—you don't 'preciate nothin'. If you had to pay a man to do de haid work dat I is doin', it would cost you fifty dollers a week—a hund'ed dollers a week—two hund'ed dollers—well, it ain't no tellin' 'cause I don't know nobody dat could do de work dat I'se doin'.

AMOS: I knows dat you is thinkin' all de time an' tryin' to do de best you kin. It jest seems like to me though dat ev'vy time sumpin's got be done 'round yere, I'se de one dat's got do it.

ANDY: Now, wait a minute—pitcher yoreself sittin' in a taxicab—de meter say $1.95. How would you feel?

AMOS: I'd feel like gittin' out.

ANDY: No, no, you is drivin' de cab.

AMOS: Oh. Den I'd feel like goin' ahaid.

ANDY: Den de man gits out de taxicab an' gives you two dollers an' tells you to keep de change—by de way, all dat comes in to de comp'ny—dem tips—'cause we is pardners, you know.

AMOS: I'll turn in ev'vy cent I gits.

ANDY: Den as dat man gits out o' de taxicab, de next man gits in it.

AMOS: Boy, we goin' make a lot o' money in de taxicab bizness, ain't we?

ANDY: You come home at night, you is got 25 or 30 dollers wid you.

AMOS: Where'd I git it from?

ANDY: You done taken in dat much.

AMOS: I done taken in 25 or 30 dollers a day, huh?

ANDY: De fust thing you know, we'll git three-four mo' taxicabs, an' de Fresh Air Taxicab Comp'ny will have mo' taxicabs dan any—well, it ain't no use to git you too much up in de air.

AMOS: Well, dat certainly do sound nice a'right.

ANDY: Now, 'cordin' to my figures yere, we'll run a cut-rate taxicab comp'ny so dat we'll git ALL de bizness—dat's de only way to do it.

AMOS: Tell me dis—kin I take Ruby Taylor out ridin' some time?

ANDY: If she's ridin' on de meter, it's a'right.

AMOS: I got let her sit down on de seat.

ANDY: Now, wait a minute—furgit 'bout Ruby Taylor—de thing you wants to remember is dis. We is in bizness, in de Fresh Air Taxicab bizness—now, let's see how much money we makes.

AMOS: Go ahaid—figger dat up.

ANDY: You knows I figgers—I is whut dey call a certiflied public re-dountant.

AMOS: Oh, you is, huh?

ANDY: Now, we'se workin' dis on de cut rate basin—lemme see yere. We'll charge 22½ cents fur de fust mile—see, I done looked all dis stuff up—I got de figgers yere. I been watchin' taxicabs ev'vday—ev'vy time I see one I look at 'em—I'se gittin' so I knows 'em now.

AMOS: Whut you goin' charge de fust mile?

ANDY: 22½ cents.

AMOS: Where I goin' git any half cents's from?

ANDY: I'll fix de meter so dat, in case de man only ride a mile, you tap de meter on top wid a little hammer an' it jumps up to 25 to make it even money.

AMOS: 25—dat's 25 cents fur de fust mile—in case I hit it wid a hammer.

ANDY: Now de question is—how much for each 'ditional.

AMOS: How much it goin' be fur whut?

ANDY: Ev'vy mile after de fust mile is goin' cost 'em so much.

AMOS: Oh, de fust mile's goin' cost 'em 22½ cents an' if I hit wid a hammer it's 25—

ANDY: I wuz jest thinkin' yere—de way we might work dis thing—instead o' havin' dat meter runnin' on de mile, might let you take a hammer an' hit dat meter ev'vy time you think you gone a mile an' let it jump up 'bout ten cents.

AMOS: Whut you mean—ev'vy time de meter changes I got hit it wid a hammer, huh?

ANDY: Den, you see, if you git somebody in de car dat looks like dey is got a lot o' money—while you is drivin', ev'vy time you think you is gone a mile, hit de meter once—den de meter will jump up ten cents—kind of turn around an' if de man is lookin' out de side o' de car, an' you see he ain't watchin' you, give de meter another crack.

AMOS: Dat wouldn't be right though. You can't do dat.

ANDY: Yeah—we better not work it dat way—dat'll mess up wid de inde-state commerce re-mission.

AMOS: Well, how much money is we goin' make—dat's de main thin'—'splain dat to me.

ANDY: Well now—'cording to my figgers yere—say we gits 25 cents fur de fust mile an' we gits

10 cents fur ev'vy mile after dat.—How many miles kin you drive a day?

AMOS: If I could git on a open road with nothin' in front o' me, I might go pretty far at dat rate.

ANDY: Lemme see—25 and 10 is 35—dat's two miles—well, now, let's say dat you went two miles—you is got 35 cents—we got figure de-a—appre-cilation on de car—say we figure de ap-pre-cilation at one cent.

AMOS: Dat's—whutever dat is—dat's one cent, ain't it? Dat makes 36 cents.

ANDY: No, no, you re-duck de 'precilation—dat makes 34 cents. Now, gasoline comes off dat yet. Figure gasoline as 2 cents—dat's-a—32 cents left. Now, de over-haid.

AMOS: Whut over-haid?

ANDY: We got 32 cents—we got city tax—dat's a cent—better figure dat at 2 cents—dat leaves 30 cents. Den we got de State tax—figure dat at 2 cents—dat's 28 cents.

AMOS: How 'bout de income tax?

ANDY: Figure dat at 3 cents—dat leaves 25 cents.

AMOS: Dat's 25 cents we got left, ain't it?

ANDY: Well now, de garage—some place to take care o' de car—figger dat at 3 cents.

AMOS: Dat leaves 22 cents, don't it?

ANDY: Now den, we got have some kind o' office—you see we got have a office fur de Fresh Air Taxi Comp'ny so people kin call us up. Figger de rent on de office at 2 cents. Dat leave us 20 cents.

AMOS: We got have a telephone in de office too, ain't we?

ANDY: Better figger de telephone in at 3 cents—dat

leaves-a—3 from 20 is-a—whut is dat?—dat's 17, dat's whut 'tis. Now, we got have a desk and some chairs in de office so dat if anybody comes down to de headquarters of de Fresh Air Taxicab Comp'ny, dey'll know dat we'se got a big place.

AMOS: How much you goin' figger dat off?

ANDY: I ought to have a big chair an' a big desk. Let's figger off 5 cents fur dat.

AMOS: Dat's five from 17, ain't it—dat leaves-2—

ANDY: Dat leaves 12 cents. Now I got git a steenographer—an' a book keeper. No. I'll keep de books an' I'll jest git a steenographer. Steenographer figger in 2 cents.

AMOS: Dat leaves 10 cents, don't it?

ANDY: Up to now, de Fresh Air Taxicab Comp'ny is got a dime.

AMOS: Whut else is got come off o' dat dime—anything?

ANDY: Well, if I git a steenographer, I got have a typewriter. Typewriter—figger dat in at 2 cents. Dat leave us 8 cents.

AMOS: We got 8 cents left, huh?

ANDY: Now, we got let ev'vybody know where we is so we got advertise. Figger advertisin' at 4 cents.

AMOS: Goin' figger advertisin' at 4 cents, huh—dat leave how much?

ANDY: Well, 4 from 8 leaves 4.

AMOS: Whut else is we got do?

ANDY: We got buy stamps to mail de letters wid—figger dat at 2 cents—dat leaves us 2 cents left.

AMOS: We got 2 cents, huh?

ANDY: Now we got have 'lectric lights—figger de

'lectricity in at one cent. Dat leaves us one cent left.

AMOS: We got one cent now huh?

ANDY: One cent—dat's all we got left.

AMOS: You kin find sumpin' fur dat cent, can't you?

ANDY: Oh yeah—license to run de taxicab—dat takes de las' cent.

AMOS: De license takes de las' cent.

ANDY: Dere goes de las' cent.

AMOS: De Fresh Air Taxicab Comp'ny.

ANDY: De overhaid certainly did eat up de money, didn't it?

AMOS: De 'spenses done run us out o' bizness, ain't dey?

ANDY: De Fresh Air Taxicab Comp'ny. We can't make no money like dat.

AMOS: No—'cordin' to dem figures ever'thing done eat up de money.

ANDY: I got it—I'll git you two hammers an' you kin hit de meter ev'vy other block.—An' if de man in de back don't like it, bus' him in de haid.

AMOS: We got do sumpin' 'bout it a'right—we can't make no money de way we been goin'.

ANDY: I'll git you a sledge hammer, dat's whut I'll git you.

AMOS: We got do sumpin' 'bout it.

XXI

Andy has made up his mind to buy a second hand touring car and organize what is to be known as the "Fresh Air Taxicab Company". As we find the boys now they are standing on a vacant lot looking at a second hand car—the owner is trying to convince them of its merits.

AMOS: De only trouble is—when Andy jest got in dere a minute ago, Mister, dat rear axle done broke right in half.
ANDY: De minute I sit down in de back seat, Mister, it went right down on de ground.
MAN: Well, I'll tell you, boys. That's what you call a drop forged axle. They're liable to drop any time. This car, though, is one of the finest things that you ever saw after she gets running.
ANDY: Oh, yeah—git it running.
MAN: Well, now, we'll start up here at the front. You take those tires, for instance—
AMOS: Dey certainly do need some air in 'em—whoever takes 'em better pump 'em up.
ANDY: Dem tires got holes in 'em, ain't dey Mister?
MAN: Well, they might be a little porous.
ANDY: Whut you mean—porous?
MAN: Might have a few holes in the tires just like the skin on your hands. Your skin is not airproof. Do you know, boys, that if you didn't

have porous skin, you couldn't live. Same way with a tire. Nothing to worry about though. Now, are you satisfied with the tires?

ANDY: Well-a—if dem is de tires dat goes on de car, we GOT be satisfied with it. We don't wants to buy no tires fur de car right away.

AMOS: Dem fo' tires you is talkin' 'bout—dem holes lets de air OUT though, don't it?

MAN: Oh yes—you wouldn't want the same old air in those tires all the time—that's what rots the tires—rubber is just the same as—well, you take your lungs for instance—if you take the same air in your lungs all the time you're liable to get whooping cough.

ANDY: De man is right about dat, Amos. I knows dat much about de human a-nit-omy.

AMOS: Well, I guess you'se right about dat air. I jest keep pumpin' 'em up—is dat it?

MAN: Whenever they get down on the rims, you can put a little air in them.

ANDY: De man is right.

MAN: You see, boys—I've got a reason for everything that I tell you. I'll explain it to you.

AMOS: Yes sah, Mister—'splain dat to us if you will, please sah.

MAN: Now, you see these tires are kind of flat. These tires are like the airship that Lindbergh flew across the ocean in. You have heard of balloon tires?

ANDY: Oh yeah—I done heerd o' balloon tires.

MAN: Well now, Lindbergh didn't fly across the ocean in no balloons—he didn't need air in his airship—so why must you have air in your tires? Common sense will tell you that.

ANDY: I'se glad you 'splained dat to Amos 'cause he don't understan' dem things like I do.
AMOS: You might be right about it but it kind of sounds funny to me—I don' know.
ANDY: Go ahaid, Mister. Let's look up under de hood dere once—lift de hood up dere.
MAN: Alright, now we'll look under the hood. There's the motor. Needs a couple of spark plugs in there. I don't know where those two spark plugs went.
ANDY: You see, Mister—we is figgerin' on usin' dis car fur a taxicab. We is startin' whut we is callin' de Fresh Air Taxi Comp'ny.
MAN: Well, if you are starting the Fresh Air Taxi Company, this is right in keeping with what you are doing. Look at the air that can get down in the motor here and give the motor fresh air.
ANDY: De gent'man is right, Amos, de gent'man is right.
MAN: I see that YOU know something about what you are buying. I don't know about this little fellow here.
AMOS: No sah, I don't know much 'bout it as Andy do but if it suit him, I guess it's a'right wid me. He is de one dat thought of ever'thing.
ANDY: Will dat motor run?
MAN: Will this motor run? Boys, I'm telling you that's one of the finest motors that ever motored anywhere.
ANDY: Whut is de replacement?
AMOS: You ain't plannin' on replacin' de motor already, is you?
MAN: You mean the *dis*-placement.

ANDY: Dat's right—whut wuz I thinkin' 'bout?—dat was a typewriter error.
MAN: Well boys, it's hard to say. You can get that up to two thousand R-F-M's. That's revolutions a minute.
ANDY: Oh yeah—I figgered dat dat was about de right number.
AMOS: Whutever dey is, dey certainly is a mess of 'em. Two thousan'—um—'m. You said sumpin' when we fust started lookin' at dis thing about de crank shaft?
ANDY: I b'lieve you said de crank shaft wuz a little bent. Where IS de crank shaft?
MAN: The crank shaft is under the motor there—you can't see it.
ANDY: Den if nobody kin see it, it ain't goin' hurt nothin'—people ain't goin' to know if de crank shaft is bent or not when dey git in de automobile.
AMOS: How 'bout dese yere fenders, Mister? Ain't dey 'bout to fall off?
ANDY: De gent'man told you dat we could tie dem fenders on dere an' dey would stay right in place.
AMOS: 'Scuse me fur astin' 'bout 'em—I was jest wonderin' if de things wuz goin' fall off or sumpin'.
ANDY: One haidlight.
MAN: You can see with one just as good as you can with two.
ANDY: Oh yeah—I jest said dat it was one good haidlight dere.
AMOS: Do you have any kind of 'lectric light bulb IN dat haidlight?

MAN: Well, there aren't any in there right now but they don't cost nothing. They change styles so often anyway you must buy them to sort of keep up with the styles.
ANDY: How is de brakes on de car—do dey work a'right?
MAN: That's one thing that the car can do—and you'll find that out—that car can stop. You boys watch the back wheels while I put on the brakes.
AMOS: Do it have dese yere now fo'-wheel brakes on de thing?
ANDY: Why don't you shut up an' let de gent'man tell you 'bout de thing?
MAN: Boys, the car has the best brakes on it that anybody would want. You don't need four-wheel brakes. For example—suppose you are driving down the street and you see a man down at the next corner holding out his hand and he wanted you for a taxicab.
ANDY: Now, git dis in yore haid, Amos—de gent'-man is 'splainin' sumpin' to you.
AMOS: I'se listenin', Mister, I'se listenin'.
ANDY: Go ahaid, Mister—now tell him again.
MAN: You are driving down the street and you see a man a block away—you want to stop—so as you get near the man, you put on your brakes. If you had on four-wheel brakes, you would stop before you got there and there you would be half a block away from the man waiting for you to come up there. Of course you could start up again but the wear and tear on stopping and starting ain't what it used to be.
ANDY: It ain't no two ways 'bout dat.
AMOS: De only reason I ast 'bout it—I wuz jest

wonderin' if you had 'em on dere, dat's all. I kin see yore point a'right. Sometimes it's kind of nice to have 'em though, I guess. I don' know.

ANDY: How many miles do you git on a gallon?

MAN: That all depends on if you are coasting, going up hill or going down hill.

ANDY: Well, as—whutever you say—

MAN: To tell you the truth, if you can coast as long as you keep your clutch in and coast along without using gas, the better off you are. You can go that way as far as you can roll.

ANDY: Now, get dat in yore haid, Amos, case you is low on gas, cut off de gas an' coast wherever you is goin'.

AMOS: 'Spose I got go up hill though.

MAN: Then give it a couple of drops of gasoline.

ANDY: You said sumpin' about de gasoline leakin'.

AMOS: De gasoline tank is kind of porous too, I guess.

MAN: Well, the reason I told you about that, you see—I thought I'd tell you everything. Now-a —You can take them holes and stop them up with some corks if you want to. On the other hand, if you want to stop by a place some time and let 'em solder a little stuff on there, that might be better.

ANDY: Yeah—we kin take care o' dat, I guess.

MAN: I'm sorry I don't have a top for the car boys. You can get a top if you want it.

ANDY: No, no—we don't want no top, Mister. You see, we is havin' whut will be de Fresh Air Taxicab Comp'ny so we can't use no top fur it.

AMOS: I wuz jest thinkin' though—case it rains, it's goin' be bad.

ANDY: We kin do like Charlie was tellin' us yesterday. You kin put a umbrella dere an' whenever it rains, open up de umbrella.

MAN: One nice thing about it, you notice here on the inside—lean over here and look in there—see I ain't got no covering on the floor in there—two—three of them boards in there are cracked a little bit—There ain't no chance of the car filling up with water in the back. In case you are out in a hard rain, the water can just run right out on the ground, you see. If those cracks weren't back there, the thing might fill up like a bath tub.

ANDY: You got some great things 'bout de car a'right. Dat's a good thing right dere.

AMOS: How much do de thing cost, Mister? How much you wants fur it?

MAN: Well, the bottom price is-a—lemme see—

ANDY: Dat's de price we want—de bottom price—if you'll let us have it.

MAN: That car will cost you eighty-five dollars as she stands.

AMOS: Whut kind o' bottom is dat—is dat rock bottom?

MAN: Well now—rock bottom on that car—that rear axle there is-a—needs a little adjusting—take it as she stands now for seventy-five dollars.

ANDY: Seventy-five dollers?

MAN: And I'm leaving it up to you because I believe you know automobiles.

ANDY: Seventy-five dollers.

AMOS: How we goin' git it away if we bought it?

ANDY: Why don't you shut up when you see me thinkin' like dis? I'se figgerin'.

AMOS: You better figger out how we goin' move it, I'll tell you dat, while you is figgerin'.
ANDY: Mister, I THINK we'll take it.
AMOS: Wait a minute yere though—we can't pay dat much cash, Mister, I'll tell you dat. We can't pay you over four-five dollers down.
ANDY: We kin pay mo' dan dat down.
AMOS: Now we can't either—I know whut I'se talkin' 'bout—we can't pay no mo' dan dat down. Will you take five dollers down an' we'll pay five dollers a week?
MAN: Well—breaks my heart to do it but I believe I'll take that.
ANDY: Let it sit yere fur a day or two den an' we'll be back an' close up de deal wid you.
MAN: Alright boys—come back then in a couple of days and I'll get out the broom and sweep it up—get it all clean for you—might rain in the meantime, sort of wash it off.
ANDY: A'right, Mister.
MAN: Well, you come back then in two days and I'll have it all ready. Breaks my heart to see that car leave me though—breaks my heart. Well, see you later, boys.
ANDY: So long, Mister.
AMOS: So long—we'll be back.
ANDY: Dat's whut you call drivin' a bargain. When I buys 'em, I buys 'em right.
AMOS: Dat man say it breaks his heart to see de car leave him—it's li'ble to break our hearts when we git it too.
ANDY: Dere you go now—startin' a argument—I 'ranges fur a car an' you start crabbin'—
AMOS: I ain't arguin'.—I ain't arguin'. . . .

XXII

Amos and Andy are seriously considering buying a car they looked at yesterday and starting the "Fresh Air Taxicab Company". As we find the boys now, they are in their room—Amos is sweeping up the room with a broom while Andy has just figured out the population of Chicago.

AMOS: You say dat dey'se three million people yere in Chicago, huh?
ANDY: Dat's right—three million people yer in de city o' Chicago.
AMOS: Where did you see dat—in de paper or sumpin'?
ANDY: I been readin' up on things like dat. If I'se goin' run a taxicab comp'ny, I got have some figures, ain't I?
AMOS: Three million people in Chicago—Um-um. Dat certainly is sumpin', ain't it?
ANDY: 'Cordin' to de figures like dat, if we open up a taxicab comp'ny, we ought to be rich in no time.
AMOS: If we kin git dem peoples to git in our taxicab, we'll make some money.
ANDY: De only trouble wid dat automobile dat we looked at yesterday—I don't think dat's goin' hold up.
AMOS: Dat thing needs a lot o' fixin' done to it. I

don't know much 'bout automobiles. I'll try to fix it but I don't know if I kin or not.

ANDY: If we buy dat automobile an' git it out in de field somewheres where we kin work on it, I think we kin fix dat thing up.

AMOS: De rear axle is broke, you know dat. When you sit down in de car, you done broke dat thing.

ANDY: De man 'splained dat to you. He told you dat dat was a drop-fo'ged axle an' it jest dropped, dat's all.

AMOS: I'll say it dropped—it dropped all over de ground, dat's whut it done done.

ANDY: De trouble is wid you—you don't know nothin' 'bout machinery. De man 'splained ever'thing to us yisterday when we wuz lookin' at de car—

AMOS: An' you kept tellin' him yes, he wuz right an' you didn't know whut he wuz talkin' 'bout—you wuz bad as I wuz.

ANDY: Now, wait a minute—if you git sarcrastic, I'll tear up de figgers yere—den we WILL be in a mess.

AMOS: Go ahaid, tear 'em up. You ain't got no figgers dere. Three million people—dat's all you got.

ANDY: I got some stuff in my haid though dat you don't know nothin' 'bout.

AMOS: Go ahaid—keep it in yore haid. You always tellin' me *I* ain't got no sense.

ANDY: Well, you AIN'T got de sense dat I got.

AMOS: I got sense enough to know though dat I didn't know whut de man wuz talkin' 'bout over dere—you didn't have dat much sense.

ANDY: I knowed ever'thing de man wuz talkin' 'bout. I kin tell you ever'thing 'bout dat car.

AMOS: Well, I tell you—when we git de car over yere den, you fix it.

ANDY: Don't worry 'bout me—I kin go out an' fix dat car right now—have it runnin' like a steam engine.

AMOS: You might have it SOUNDIN' like a steam engine but I bet you can't git it runnin'.

ANDY: De trouble is wid you—you don't 'preciates whut I'se doin' fur you.

AMOS: I 'preciates it a'right—de only thing, I don't want you to keep tellin' me I ain't no sense ev'vy day. I got some pride de same as you is. De way YOU talks to me sometimes, makes me feel like I ain't nothin'. If I lissen to you all day long, I'll feel like jumpin' out de window or sumpin'. Why don't you say sumpin' GOOD about me sometime?

ANDY: Now lissen Amos—come yere—sit down—unlax yoreself, unlax yoreself.

AMOS: I'se unlaxed—I'se a'right. De only thing—you hurts my feelin's some times, Andy. I know I ain't smart but I got SOME sense an' you keep tellin' me I ain't got NO sense.

ANDY: De trouble is wid you, you don't think.

AMOS: Well, I TRIES to think. I thinks sometime. I don' always say ever'thing I'se thinkin'.

ANDY: Well, maybe dat's de trouble wid me—I don' know. Maybe I tells you too much.

AMOS: No, I don' mind listenin' to you when you'se tellin' me things—but you'se always tellin' me how dumb I is an' ever'thing—you hurts my pride.

ANDY: No—de trouble wid me is, I guess,—I tells you too much—I talks too much to you. You see, I knows you is a'right. De trouble is—yore haid is like a bucket.—I kin pour water out o' my haid in yore haid like a bucket—but after I pour so much, den yore haid is full. Den whut I ought to do, I ought to wait till whut I is done poured in yore haid is done had time to e-vap-o-late—den give you another shot. But, instead o' doin' dat, I'se tellin' you stuff faster dan you kin 'sorb it.

AMOS: I'se willin' to do anything to try to git along an' understan' it—I'll work like a dog an' ever'thing else. De only thing—I DO hates fur you to keep on jumpin' on me.

ANDY: Now, don't git all worked up. Un-lax again. Stay un-laxed.

AMOS: I'm a'right—I'm gittin' along a'right—Jest don't say no mo' to me 'bout bein' dumb, will you? Some o' dese days I goin' show you dat I ain't as dumb as you thinks I is.

ANDY: When I say you'se dumb, I don' mean you'se dumb lak a dog.

AMOS: I'se glad you don' mean dat.

ANDY: I jest mean dat you is thick-headed, dat's all.

AMOS: Now, dere you go again, you see. Dat's whut hurts me, Andy, when you talks to me like dat. I can't help it if I wuzn't born wid all kind o' brains like big mens is.

ANDY: Now, wait a minute—don't start cryin'.

AMOS: I know—you tell me not to start cryin'—den you talk to me like dat—I got feelin's same as you is—how would you like somebody talkin' to you tellin' you dey was sumpin' wrong wid you all de time like dat dat you couldn't help? Whut kin I do 'bout it?

ANDY: Well, it ain't nothin' you kin do 'bout it, Amos.

AMOS: Well, whut you wants to keep on jumpin' on me like dat den fur? I tries not to git mad. Ever'thing you done told me—I listens to it but I'se jest lak a dog or anything else. You can't keep on beatin' a dog—some day dat dog goin' turn on you. Down in de dog's heart, he might love you but if you keep on beatin' him —an' he loves you jest de same—but he goin' turn on you.

ANDY: I ain't beatin' you—I ain't tryin' to beat you.

AMOS: No, you ain't beatin' me wid yore fist—you ain't tryin' to beat me wid yore fist—but you'se beatin' at my heart—dat's whut you'se beatin' at. Dat's de worst kin' o' beatin' anybody kin take too.

ANDY: Come yere now, Amos—come on now—don't feel dat way.

AMOS: It's easy enough fur you to tell me not to feel dat way but when somebody's always cuttin' you like dey'se cuttin' you wid a knife— hurtin' yore feelin's an' hurtin' yore pride an' ever'thing else, it ain't so easy to say—"let's furgit it."

ANDY: Ain't I yore buddy?

AMOS: You is my buddy a'right, Andy, an' I is yore buddy too, I hopes. Dat's why I can't understan' sometimes de way you jump on me. Some time I think dat if you did love me down in yore heart, you wouldn't talk to me de way you do.

ANDY: Amos, ev'vy time I talk to you like dat, it's fur yore own good.

AMOS: I knows you tries to do things fur me—I knows you try to help me. I b'lieve you'd do anything in de world fur me if it come right down to it. I don't care whut anybody say, I b'lieve if somebody bigger dan I wuz, jumped on me, I b'lieve you'd jump in dere an' help me if it killed you—an' I'd do de same thing fur you, Andy—but please don't talk 'bout me no mo' dat hurts my feelin's, will you?

ANDY: Well, you knows I'se sorry if I hurt yore feelin's.

AMOS: Don't think dat I'se a big baby 'cause I'se standin' yere wid tears in my eyes. Nobody'll ever know how I feel till dey feels like I do.

ANDY: Well now lissen, Amos—from now on, I'se goin' try not to hurt yore feelin's.

AMOS: If you'd jest do dat much fur me, I certainly will 'preciate it, Andy. I'll do anything in de world fur you if you'll jest do dat much. And another thing, you knows I'se in love wid Mamie down in Atlanta—don't say no mo' 'bout her, will you? If you don't lak her, jest don't say nothin' 'bout her.

ANDY: I laks Mamie a'right.

AMOS: No, I don't think you DO lak her. I wish you did. But do me a favor an' don't say no mo' to me now. If you wants to go in de taxicab bizness, I'll go wid you. I'll work day an' night till I drop in my tracks. I'll do anything.

ANDY: Amos, from now on, I goin' be better to you.

AMOS: I don't wants you to be better—I jest don't want you to call me no more names or say

ANDY: Well, now lissen, Amos—from now on, I'se goin' try not to hurt yore feelin's.

AMOS: If you'd jest do dat much fur me, I certainly will 'preciate it, Andy.

nothin' to me to hurt me, dat's all. I'll try to learn ever'thing as fast as I kin an' I'll work my haid off. I don't know whut is de matter wid me today—I'se jest kind of homesick an' lonesome—I'se jest kind of down in de dumps, dat's all.

ANDY: Come on—put on yore hat—let's go out an' git some fresh air.

AMOS: I don't care—I'll walk around wid you an' git a little fresh air. But don't be mad wid me now 'cause I said dat—I jest had to git it off my chest, dat's all.

ANDY: Come on—we'll go down an' see a movin' pitcher show or sumpin'—dat'll make you feel better—put yore arm around me.

AMOS: I'se wid you—come on.

XXIII

Amos and Andy finally decided to buy the second hand automobile and start a taxi company. As we find the boys now they are standing near the car which they just purchased for $75.00, on the instalment plan,—the car is sitting on a vacant lot in what a mechanic would call "a pretty bad condition".

AMOS: Well, we got it—yere 'tis—we done paid five dollers down on it.
ANDY: Amos, we is now in de taxicab bizness. De Fresh Air Taxicab Company. I don't know if we ought to git incorpulated today or wait a few days.
AMOS: Will it help us any if we git dat done to us?
ANDY: Well, if we incor-pulates, we is always got de corpulation back of us.
AMOS: Whut you mean, we got de corpulation back of us?
ANDY: Well, yere's de automobile.
AMOS: Yeah, yere's de automobile—I 'grees wid you dere—we got dat a'right.
ANDY: Now, de nex' thing we is goin' in de taxicab bizness. 'Spose we has a accident. If we is incorpulated, we don't have to worry—let de corpulation worry. Dat's de 'vantage o' doin' dat.

Amos: Dat's a good idea a'right. I guess we ought to git incor-pulated.
Andy: Jest think, Amos—yere we is in Chicago—we ain't been yere but about six weeks an' already we is got a automobile. Whut would de boys down in Atlanta say if dey could see us up yere wid our automobile?
Amos: I feel like I is rich, you know it?
Andy: I'll have to write a letter to some o' de boys down dere an' tell 'em dat we is opened a taxicab comp'ny.
Amos: Yeah—we might do a little advertisin' down dere in case any o' de boys come up yere to Chicago, we'll tell 'em dat we'll meet 'em at de depot an' take 'em 'round wherever dey wants us to take 'em.
Andy: Any time any o' de boys come up yere from Atlanta, we'll git 'em to use de Fresh Air Taxicab.
Amos: We could give 'em a little discount.
Andy: I ain't givin' nobody no discount. If any of our friends git in dat thing, we wants to sock it to 'em.
Amos: I wish de automobile had a top on it.
Andy: Dere you go now—you'se tryin' to ruin de whole thing. Whut you 'spose I named de comp'ny de Fresh Air Taxi Comp'ny fur? IF we had a top on de car, dat would kill de whole idea. People kin git in dis taxicab, sit dere in de sunshine out in de air—dat is one o' de greates' things dat is ever been 'vented—whut I jest done.
Amos: Oh, I 'grees wid you dere a'right.
Andy: Well, yere we is—we got de automobile.

Amos: De nex' thing is movin' it.

Andy: Now, I is gonna 'point you as de chief mechanic's mate—you has charge of all de machinery—you gits ever'thing in workin' order—den I'll 'spect it—see if it's a'right.

Amos: Well, de fust thing we got do is to git it off dis lot, ain't we?

Andy: De fust thing we ought to do is ride around de block in it to see if ever'thing's a'right.

Amos: Dat's whut we ought to done befo' we bought it, I guess.

Andy: Dere you go now—findin' fault.

Amos: I ain't findin' fault—I'se jest said I thought maybe we ought to tried de thing out 'fore we bought it.

Andy: Is de gasoline tank got any gasoline in it?

Amos: Mr. Jarvis said dat it had 'bout half a gallon o' gasoline in it. A little rain done got in de gasoline tank though an' dere's *some* water in dere.

Andy: Dere's a idea right dere—we kin mix a little water wid de gasoline—we ain't got feed dis car pure gasoline.

Amos: Will water and gasoline mix?

Andy: If you git it in a bottle an' shake it up, it'll mix.

Amos: I wonder if de car's got any oil in it?

Andy: Lif' up de hood—let's take a look at it.

Amos: Where is de oil place on yere dat you pours de oil in?

Andy: Lay de top back down dere now so it ain't goin' drop down on me—lay it down—dat's de stuff.

Amos: Whut is dese two holes yere—is dat where you puts de oil?

Andy: Dat oil dere is fur de spark plugs. We is short two spark plugs. She ain't hittin' on but two cylinders.

Amos: She ain't hittin' on none yet, is she? She ain't hittin' on nothin'.

Andy: We kin run de thing on two cylinders after we git it goin' till we git enough money to buy a couple mo' spark plugs.

Amos: I wonder where you find out about oil on de thin'?

Andy: De thing MUST have oil in it.

Amos: If you think it's got it in dere, we'll furgit 'bout de oil den.

Andy: Ain't no use to worry 'bout de oil. De thing is GOT have oil in it. Automobiles can't run widout oil an' dey run de thing up yere where it is now so oil don't e-vap-o-late—so it must be some still in dere.

Amos: Well, whut is we goin' do wid de automobile now?

Andy: Well-a—if I git you a hammer an' a screw driver, do you thinks you kin git it in workin' re-dition by—well, say, in a hour?

Amos: Better not count on gittin' me no hammer an' screw driver—I don't know if I goin' need dem or not. I tell you whut though—I don't care whut Mr. Jarvis say about dem tires—seems to me dey ought to have some air in 'em—dey is right down on de rims now.

Andy: Mr. Jarvis told you dat de tires was porous tires—dey had a few air holes in 'em—dat ain't goin' hurt nothin'. Whut is you lookin' under de car 'bout?

Amos: Look yere—wait a minute—something on the ground under de car—I'll reach under dere an' git it.

Andy: Whut is you gittin' from under de car now?

Amos: Look yere—yere's a cog wheel an' two—three nuts an' dis yere bolt. Is dey done fell out de car?

Andy: Dat thing didn't come out de car, did it?

Amos: He was tellin' us sumpin' 'bout de bottom o' de car when I looked under it—I furgit whut he said though.

Andy: Oh, I 'members whut he said now—he said dat he didn't have no dust-pan under dere. We kin go to de five an' ten cents sto' an' git a dust pan. De best thing to do though, instead o' dustin' de car off is to git a damp rag an' wipe it off.

Amos: Well, I wonder where dis yere cog wheel come from an' dese yere bolts?

Andy: Dat couldn't come out de motor.

Amos: De motor is cracked, you know—it's got a great big crack runnin' right across de top of it.

Andy: Wait a minute—lemme git in dis driver's seat yere.

Amos: Whut's de matter—won't dat door open?

Andy: Well, I be doggoned—de door's nailed shut.

Amos: I wonder if de door in de back seat is de same way? If it is, we got cut a hole through dere so de people kin git in it.

Andy: See if you kin open de back door dere. Pull hard, pull hard.

Amos: One side of it will open but dis side won't.

ANDY: *Pull* on de thing.
AMOS: I'se pullin'. LOOKOUT!

ANDY: *Pull* on de thing!
AMOS: (pulling) I'se pullin'. LOOKOUT!
ANDY: Look at you now, look at you.
AMOS: Well I be doggoned—I done pull de door off de hinges.
ANDY: Whut you tryin' to do?—pull de car to pieces? We jest got de thing an' now you tryin' to break it up.
AMOS: You tol' me to pull on de car though—dat's whut you tol' me to do.
ANDY: Lay de do' in de back seat now—dat's sumpin' else we got fix. Lemme step over de front door now an' git in de driver's seat.
AMOS: Go ahaid—sit down in de driver's seat—see how it feels.
ANDY: Wait a minute yere—I can't git my knees down under dis thing.
AMOS: Whut's de matter?—You'se kind of tangled up dere, ain't you?
ANDY: Wait a minute—come up yere—help me! I got my foot yere tangled up wid de 'mergency brake.
AMOS: Wait a minute—I'll pull yore foot out.
ANDY: OW! Don't bend my foot 'round dat way— Un-lease de brake—un-lease de brake!
AMOS: It mus' be stuck.
ANDY: So is my foot. Take off de clutch or sumpin'.
AMOS: Whut you mean—take it off de automobile?
ANDY: Un-lease it, un-lease it.
AMOS: Ever'thing IS un-leased.
ANDY: My foot ain't un-leased—can't you see de thing stuck in dere. Yere, now put yore hand under my knee dere. Now, pull it up—UP! dat's de stuff.

Amos: I be doggoned—done pulled yore shoe off.
Andy: Reach down dere an' git my shoe out o' dat mess.
Amos: Wait a minute—I'll git it fur you—yere 'tis. You kind of be careful 'bout dat.
Andy: I don't see how *I* goin' drive dis car 'less I hang my feet over, de side while I'se drivin'. Yere—slip dat shoe on dat foot.
Amos: Hold still. If you had some feet in yore socks, yore foot would go in yere better.
Andy: Dat's enough—dat's enough—now wait a minute—lemme see yere—where is de 'nition?
Amos: Whut is you lookin' fur?
Andy: De switch dat turns on de 'nition.
Amos: Whut is dis yere thing?
Andy: Wait a minute—lemme see—whut is dat?—L-i-g-h—oh, dat's lights, dat's whut dat is. Git up front—when I switch dis—see if de lights go on.
Amos: Ain't no use to watch de lights 'cause we ain't got no globes in dat headlight.
Andy: Whut you mean, ain't no bulb in de thing?
Amos: Dat's right—ain't no globe in it—den de wires is kind of broke too.
Andy: Well, watch it anyway—see if anything happens. I goin' turn it now—yere it goes. Anything happen?
Amos: Ain't nothin' happened yet. Switch it again.
Andy: I'll turn it back now—see if dey go out. Dere it is—did dey go out?
Amos: Dey ain't been on yet.
Andy: Well, dat needs fixin'.
Amos: If you wants to try it again, I'll watch it.
Andy: Wait a minute—ain't no use to wear yoreself

[160]

out watchin' dat. See if de tail light goes on when I switch dis thing?

AMOS: Wait till I git back dere.

ANDY: Did it go on?

AMOS: Ain't no tail light on yere.

ANDY: See any wire stickin' out anywhere?

AMOS: No, de fender's got a hole in it back yere—you kin hang a red light on de back of it if you wants to—a lamp—one o' dem oil lamps.

ANDY: Yere's de switch—startin' switch—yere—yere—see yere—say-a—s-t-a-r-t start.

AMOS: Whut is you goin' do—start de car runnin' now?

ANDY: Now, wait a minute—I'se goin' throw dis on start—see whut happens.

AMOS: You better git ready to cut it off right quick case she starts runnin'.

ANDY: Look out now—I goin' throw it over on start—dere she is—whut happened?

AMOS: I heard sumpin'.

ANDY: Whut did you hear?

AMOS: Wait a minute—I hear sumpin' under de car.

ANDY: See whut 'tis.

AMOS: Look yere! Another cog wheel done fell out.

ANDY: WHUT kind o' mess is dis anyway?

AMOS: Look out! Dere comes some bolts fallin'—look at de stuff comin' out now—

XXIV

As we find the boys tonight they are in their room seated at a table—Andy has just elected himself president of the new taxicab company while Amos is still a little bewildered to know how the election got by so quickly.

Amos: You say dat you is done been 'lected to de president of de comp'ny, huh?
Andy: Amos—you is done heard de pros an' connies of de whole thing right yere in front of you.
Amos: Whut you mean—de pros an' connies—I don't know nothin' 'bout dat. You say you is de president of de comp'ny—is dat whut you say?
Andy: We jest dis minute had a meetin' wid all de officers an' de stock-holders an' ever'body else was yere an' I wuz 'lected president.
Amos: I b'lieve you is seein' things, you know it?
Andy: Whut you mean, you b'lieve I is seein' things? Don't 'sult de president. Yere I is an' ain't been in office over three minutes an' one o' de 'ployees is 'sultin' me.
Amos: I ain't tryin' to 'sult you but ain't nobody been yere but me an' you and you say all de officers an' stock holders was yere.
Andy: Lissen yere—when you hold a bizness meetin' like we jest had yere, you always says "Gent'-

mens, stock-holders, officers" when you redress 'em.

AMOS: But de trouble is, dey ain't nobody been yere but jest de two of us.

ANDY: You ain't goin' start no argument now 'bout dis, is you? I is been 'lected president of de comp'ny. Nobody 'posed me.

AMOS: You ain't give nobody a chance to 'pose you yet.

ANDY: You ain't tryin' to run again me fur de president, is you?

AMOS: No, I ain't tryin' to run again you fur president. Dat ain't whut I'se talkin' 'bout.

ANDY: Whut IS you talkin' 'bout?

AMOS: How do *I* come out—whut is I?

ANDY: Well now—NOW dat's diff'ent. I is de president, ain't I? De president of de Fresh Air Taxicab Comp'ny of America incorpulated.

AMOS: How do I come out now—w-w-whut do dat make me?

ANDY: You don't know nothin' 'bout shorthand, do you?

AMOS: I don't know NOTHIN' 'bout shorthand.

ANDY: I wuz goin' give you de honor o' bein' de secketary to de president but you don't wants to git messed up in dat.

AMOS: I ought to be sumpin' myself.

ANDY: How would you like to be de treasurer—no, wait a minute—dat's bad—dat's money.

AMOS: I'd like to be sumpin' dat kind of 'mounts to sumpin'.

ANDY: Well, you know, you is de one dat's goin' drive de taxicab. Dat is sumpin' even if you don't have no name. Dat's a big thing right dere.

AMOS: I know—but I'd like to have some name so dat when somebody ast me whut I is, I kin tell 'em.

ANDY: Well, lemme see now—I is de president of de Fresh Air Taxicab Comp'ny. By de way, where is de taxicab?

AMOS: It's still settin' out on dat vacant lot over dere.

ANDY: Anything wrong wid it?

AMOS: Ever'thing.

ANDY: Wait a minute yere. I can't be de president of a taxicab comp'ny if de taxicab ain't in good shape. Whut's wrong wid it?

AMOS: Well, it ain't got no tires on it—it ain't got no lights on it—de gasoline tank got holes in it—de fenders is 'bout to fall off—ain't got no top on it an' it won't run.

ANDY: Needs fixin', don't it?

AMOS: Needs a MESS o' fixin'.

ANDY: I got it.

AMOS: You got whut?

ANDY: I got a name fur you whut you kin be in de comp'ny.

AMOS: Whut kin I be?

ANDY: Boy, I'm goin' give you a name yere dat will knock you dead. When de peoples heah whut YOU is, dey goin' sit up an take notice.

AMOS: Now you is comin'—whut is I goin' be?

ANDY: I is goin' call you Chief Mechanic's Mate, Fixer of Automobile, Haid Driver of de comp'ny and Chief Bizness Getter.

AMOS: Boy, dat is a name right dere now. Now I

done got myself a name. When I write Mamie a letter an' she heahs about dat name—dat's goin' be too bad. Um—um—whut is dat again?

ANDY: You ain't done furgit it, is you?

AMOS: When you wuz callin' all dem big names, my heart went right up in my mouth, an' I couldn't think about whut you wuz sayin'—I wuz so 'cited.

ANDY: De only trouble is—I'se 'fraid I is givin' you too much of a name dere—you'se li'ble to git de swell haid or sumpin'—think you is bigger dan I is.

AMOS: I ain't goin' git de swell haid—ain't no danger o' me gittin' de swell haid.

ANDY: Now, lemme write dis down on a piece o' paper dis time. De Fresh Air Taxicab Comp'ny of America—now, write dat down yere—de—fresh—air—T-a-x-y—taxi—cab comp'ny—of—America.

AMOS: Now you goin' write down *my* name, ain't you?

ANDY: Now, look dere, dat's jest whut I tol' you—you thinks you is bigger dan I is already. I come down yere fust—I is de president of de comp'ny. Andrew—Brown, President.

AMOS: Ain't you goin' call yoreself Andy?

ANDY: You kin call me Andy when you'se talkin' to me but when I put my name down as president of de comp'ny, I calls myself Andrew.

AMOS: Den I come nex' don't I?

ANDY: Amos—Jones—

AMOS: Now whut is I again now?

ANDY: Let's see now—'fore I write it down yere you is-a—Chief Mechanic's Mate—Fixer of

Automobile—Haid Driver of de comp'ny an' Chief Bizness Getter.

Amos: Dat certainly is a mess o' names I got, ain't it?

Andy: Now, we'll write dat down—Chief—Mechanic's Mate—Fixer of Automobile—Haid Driver of de comp'ny—an' Chief Bizness Getter.

Amos: Um—um—dat certainly is sumpin'—look dere.

Andy: But don't furgit one thing, Amos—wid all dem names, you ain't as big as I is 'cause I is de president.

Amos: Oh, I don't care how BIG I is—I jest wants to call myself sumpin' so when I write to Mamie or if Ruby Taylor asts me, dey'll think dat I IS somebody.

Andy: Now den—de comp'ny is organ-rised. Ever'thing is ready.

Amos: De automobile ain't ready yet.

Andy: Well, wait a minute yere—dat comes under you—dat is in yore 'partment.

Amos: Whut you mean—dat comes under me?

Andy: Look yere whut you is—look at dis piece o' paper yere.

Amos: 'Splain dat to me—whut you mean yere?

Andy: Well, de fust thing you is—you is de Chief Mechanic's Mate.

Amos: Whut is dat got do wid fixin' a automobile?

Andy: Well, dat's whut you IS.

Amos: Dat's whut I is whut?

Andy: De Chief Mechanic's Mate.

Amos: Well, dat's whut I ast you? Whut is dat got

do wid fixin' de automobile? I can't fix de automobile by myself.

ANDY: You don't 'speck de president of de comp'ny to fix de automobile, do you? Who ever heerd of de president of de comp'ny layin' under a automobile.

AMOS: I don't mind layin' under a automobile—I'll lay under dere—but dat ain't goin' do no good—jest layin' under dere—you got hammer on de thing.

ANDY: Well, git yoreself a hammer.

AMOS: De trouble is—I don't know whut to hit.

ANDY: If you hit yoreself in de haid a couple o' times, it might help you some. I told you dat you could git a hammer an' a screw driver.

AMOS: Whut good is a hammer an' a screw driver goin' do me?

ANDY: Tain't no use to argue wid you—if you don't git better dan you is, I goin' take all dem names away from you.

AMOS: Don't take dem names away from me now—you jest gimme dem names.

ANDY: Well den—git a hammer an' try to fix de automobile.

AMOS: Well, de way dat automobile is standin' dere now, it's goin' take somebody dat knows more dan I do to fix it.

ANDY: Den I see de president of de comp'ny is gonna have to go out an' fix de car. Dat's a dis-re-grace though to have de president doin' work like dat.

AMOS: Well, I don't wants to dis-re-grace you.

ANDY: I done give you all dem names but if you

don't back it up by doin' sumpin' whut's de use o' foolin' de people?

AMOS: Dat car's in a bad fix though right now. Dat's goin' need a lot o' work on it.

ANDY: Well, dat's whut you'se 'sposed to do.

AMOS: To tell you de truth though, Andy, I don't think I knows how to fix it.

ANDY: Is you got any money?

AMOS: I ain't got much money—you know tomorrow's pay day—I got about seventy cents left out o' de money dat I borrowed from one o' de boys down dere.

ANDY: Go down to de five an' ten cents sto' an' git me a hammer, a screw driver, an' a piece o' rope—I'll fix dat car.

AMOS: A'right—I'll go on down an' git you dat stuff at de five an' ten cent sto'.

XXV

Amos and Andy are still working on the construction job, thinking it best not to quit until they can get the second hand car in good shape and ready for business. In order to speed up the repairing of the automobile, they gave the job to a young boy who lives across the street from them. This young boy, who is known as Sylvester, agreed to work without any salary until the taxicab company gets on a paying basis. As the scene opens now we find Amos and Andy just arriving at the spot where Sylvester has been working on the car all day. Much to their surprise Sylvester has apparently taken the motor to pieces and piled it up on the ground.

AMOS: Well, I be doggoned—whut is goin' on yere?
ANDY: Whut in de world IS you doin' dere, Sylvester, wid dat automobile?
SYL: Hello, Mr. Andy—Hello, Mr. Amos—I'se tryin' to git de car runnin'.
ANDY: You can't git de thing runnin' wid all de runnin' stuff layin' out yere on de ground like dat.
SYL: Well, I tell you whut I thought, Mr. Andy—I thought de fust thing I'd do would be to clean de car.
ANDY: CLEAN de car?
AMOS: How come you take all dis yere stuff out o'

de car an' pile it up on de ground like dat, Sylvester?

ANDY: I'se re-gusted.

SYL: Well, I tell you de truth, gent'men—I was talkin' to my papa an' you know he works in a boiler fact'ry an' he told me de best thing to do was to knock ever'thing out o' de car fust.

ANDY: KNOCK ever'thing out de car? You don't mean to tell de president of de comp'ny yere dat you is done *knocked* dat stuff out?

SYL: I didn't knock it all out—most of it fell out.

ANDY: I'se re-gusted.

AMOS: De funny part of it is—I don't think we goin' ever be able to git it back.

ANDY: You don't THINK we goin' ever be able —I KNOW we ain't—'less I start figgerin' it out myself.

SYL: Well, you gent'mens ain't mad jest 'cause I took de motor to pieces, is you?

AMOS: No—we ain't mad—

ANDY:—Shut up. *I* is de one dat gits mad 'round yere when anything happens—I is de president. —I don't know if I'se mad or not.

AMOS: De main thing is gittin' all dem parts back in de motor, ain't it?

ANDY: Sylvester, whut in de world is you doin' takin' all dem things out?

SYL: Well, I tell you, Mr. Andy—I wuz talkin' to my Gram'ma las' night an' I told her I wuz goin' work fur you gent'mens today.

ANDY: You wuz talkin' to yore Gram'ma?

SYL: Yas sah—I told her dat I wuz goin' help you fix yore automobile—an' Gram'ma tol' me to take it to pieces fust an' clean ever'thing.

ANDY: Is yore Gram'ma a mechanic?
AMOS: Do yore Gram'ma know anything about automobiles, Sylvester?
SYL: You see—It sort o' runs in de fam'ly. My papa used to work in a boiler factory an' my Gram'ma used to fix his lunch fur him ev'vyday.
ANDY: You better git yore Gram'ma over yere to fix dis car.
AMOS: I think we kin git dem parts back in dere after we git a book o' 'structions.
ANDY: It would take fo'teen men ten years to git dat car back together, de way it look to me. I'se re-gusted. Yere I is—de president of de Fresh Air Taxicab Comp'ny—thinkin' dat de taxicab is ready to start runnin'—an' I come over an' find it layin' on de ground.
AMOS: It's a funny thing to me—
ANDY: Whut's so funny 'bout it?
AMOS: It's jest a funny thing whut makes a automobile run.
ANDY: I'se re-gusted.
SYL: I hope you gent'mens ain't mad wid me fur doin' dis.
AMOS: Oh no, Sylvester—don you worry—you doin' de best you kin. Another thing, Andy, you know Sylvester's workin' fur nothin'.
ANDY: De trouble is though—we got pay two men to put de car back together so we is losin'—I'd make money if I paid Sylvester not to touch de car.
SYL: I hope you ain't mad wid me, Mr. Andy—
ANDY: Well, you know I is de president of de comp'ny an' all this falls on my shoulders.
AMOS: Let's see if we can't get de car back together.

ANDY: Yeah, don't pull no mo' stuff out dere. Tell yore Gram'ma when you go home dat you done done enough cleanin'.

AMOS: Now, let's see—whut goes where.

ANDY: Wait a minute now—'fore you start on dat mess—lemme look over it yere.

AMOS: You is president of de comp'ny—you go ahaid, look it over befo' we start puttin' it back together.

ANDY: Dis certainly is a mess. Let me walk around and look dis car over—I want to 'spect it.

AMOS: Where did you git dat stove pipe from?

SYL: Dat ain't no stove pipe—dat's de exhaust pipe.

AMOS: Is dat whut dat thing is?

ANDY: Whut is dese things right yere?

SYL: Dat is de timin' gear.

ANDY: Oh yeah—dat's whut I thought dat wuz. Is dat got a clock in it?

SYL: No sah, no sah—dat ain't got no clock—I'll 'splain it to you.

ANDY: No, no—dat's a'right—don't tell de president.

AMOS: Dis yere thing didn't come out dere, did it?

SYL: Yas sah, Mr. Amos—dat's de manifold.

AMOS: You don't mean to tell me.

ANDY: Anybody knows dat, Amos.

AMOS: I jest happened to ast him whut it wuz—I didn't know myself.

ANDY: Lemme look de rest of de car over yere (fading out a little) Well, I see you didn't take de seats out o' de car—dey is still in dere.

AMOS: It certainly is a lot o' stuff piled up yere. All dat come out de motor, huh?

ANDY: It look like two—three motors is layin' dere to me.
AMOS: If we didn't pay but seventy-five dollers fur dis car an' it had all dat stuff in it, I think we got a pretty good bargain.
ANDY: Well, yere we is wid all de stuff.
SYL: You'se goin' have to buy some new pistons.
ANDY: I don' wants no pistols.
AMOS: No, we don't wants to mess 'round wid no pistols or guns or nothin', Sylvester.
SYL: No sah, whut I say—I say you got buy some new pistons—an' piston rings.
ANDY: We got BUY some, huh? Whut we goin' do wid 'em?
SYL: Well, if you don't git some, de cylinders is goin' leak oil.
ANDY: If we don't put no oil in dere, it ain't goin' leak oil. Dat's one thing we kin do.
AMOS: We got figure out sumpin' yere.
ANDY: Yere I is—de president o' de Fresh Air Taxicab Comp'ny—thinkin' dat de automobile was ready to run—an' yere it is layin' all over de ground.
SYL: If you want me to let it alone, Mr. Andy—I'll do dat.
ANDY: Well, as long as you started on de thing, ain't no use to quit—but I better super-ize de job from now on myself.
AMOS: You goin' to do de work yoreself Andy?
ANDY: I ain't goin' do de work but I goin' tell Sylvester whut to do yere.
AMOS: I'se hungry—I'd like to git sumpin' to eat— we ain't had no supper yet, you know.
ANDY: You ain't no hungrier dan I is. You know I

been workin' all day over on dat buildin' same as you is.

AMOS: Well, if you wants to, you go ahead an' eat an' me an' Sylvester will stay yere an' work on de car till you come back.

SYL: Yas sah, yas sah, we do dat.

ANDY: I better not leave you two boys yere on dat car—you is li'ble to take de body to pieces while I'se gone.

AMOS: Well, whut is we goin' do yere?

ANDY: De fust thing we wants to do is git de motor back together.

AMOS: Well, if you want us to, we'll hand you de-a —dese yere wheels an' things an' you kin put 'em back in de car, Andy.

ANDY: Now, wait a minute yere—lemme do a little thinkin' a minute.

AMOS: How's ever'thing, Sylvester?

SYL: Ever'thing's a'right, Mr. Amos. Did you see Ruby Taylor today?

AMOS: No, I ain't seed her.

ANDY: Dere you go now—talkin' 'bout gals—yere we is wid de automobile layin' out on de ground an' you boys talkin' 'bout Ruby Taylor.

AMOS: We jest happened to speak o' her—dat's all we done.

ANDY: Lemme see yere now. Yere is de automobile all de nuts an' wheels an' ever'thing is layin' out on de ground—whut is de nex' thing to do?

AMOS: Git 'em back in de car.

ANDY: Don't try to tell de president whut to do.

AMOS: I thought you ast me whut to do.

SYL: Well, I tell you, Mr. Andy—

ANDY: Shut up—both o' you. I'll figger dis thing out. Lemme see—de Fresh Air Taxicab Comp'ny—it certainly is a mess now.

CPSIA information can be obtained
at www.ICGtesting.com
Printed in the USA
BVHW031015061222
653561BV00011B/147